Before the Millennium

Karim Khan

methuen | drama

LONDON • NEW YORK • OXFORD • NEW DELHI • SYDNEY

METHUEN DRAMA

Bloomsbury Publishing Plc, 50 Bedford Square, London, WC1B 3DP, UK
Bloomsbury Publishing Inc, 1359 Broadway, New York, NY 10018, USA
Bloomsbury Publishing Ireland, 29 Earlsfort Terrace, Dublin 2,
D02 AY28, Ireland

BLOOMSBURY, METHUEN DRAMA and the Methuen
Drama logo are trademarks of Bloomsbury Publishing Plc.

First published in Great Britain 2025

A catalogue record for this book is available from the British Library.

A catalog record for this book is available from the Library of Congress.

ISBN: PB: 978-1-3506-1405-5
ePDF: 978-1-3506-1406-2
eBook: 978-1-3506-1407-9

Series: Modern Plays

Typeset by Mark Heslington Ltd, Scarborough, North Yorkshire

For product safety related questions contact
productsafety@bloomsbury.com.

To find out more about our authors and books visit
www.bloomsbury.com and sign up for our newsletters.

Before the Millennium was first presented at the Old Fire Station, Oxford, on 1 December 2025.

Cast (in order of appearance)

Zoya – Gurjot Dhaliwal

Iqra – Prabhleen Oberoi

Faiza – Hannah Khalique-Brown

Company

Director – Adam Karim

Set and Costume Designer – Maariyah Sharjil

Lighting Designer – Holly Ellis

Composer and Sound Designer – XANA

Movement Director – Rakhee Sharma

Dramaturg – Gurnesha Bola

Dialect Coach – Gurkiran Kaur

Producer – Jessie Anand

Production Manager – Dan Knight

Stage Manager – Olivia Wolfenden

Zoya – Gurjot Dhaliwal

Gurjot Dhaliwal is a London-based actor who trained at the Royal Central School of Speech and Drama (2021). Her previous stage credits include: *Our White Skoda Octavia* (Touring), *Shewolves* (Southwark Playhouse) and *Asian Girls in Therapy* (VAULT Festival). Screen credits include: *Sweetpea* (Sky Atlantic), *Mr Bigstuff* (Sky) and *Extraordinary* (Disney+). Her self-written and performed in short film *Pink or Blue* (Rifco) premiered at London Indian Film Festival 2025.

Iqra – Prabhleen Oberoi

Prabhleen Oberoi is a London-based actress, dancer, and award-winning choreographer. A recent graduate of the Oxford School of Drama, her screen and stage credits include work for *EastEnders*, Netflix, Kylie Minogue and The Jonas Brothers. She recently made waves as the Commercial Bollywood Choreographer for BBC's *Strictly Come Dancing*. Holding a degree from the London School of Economics, Prabhleen is passionate about championing brown artistry and exploring stories that celebrate shared humanity.

Faiza – Hannah Khalique-Brown

Hannah can next be seen reprising her lead role of Saara Parvin in the second season of Channel 4/Peacock's *The Undeclared War* opposite Simon Pegg for showrunner Peter Kosminsky. Hannah's performance in S1 drew unanimous critical claim including 'Khalique-Brown, a newcomer is sensational' (New Statesman), 'Khalique-Brown gives a masterclass in restrained acting' (The Times), 'there are few experienced actors who can share a scene with Rylance and not disappear and Khalique-Brown holds her own' (Sunday Times).

Hannah continued her brilliant relationship with Kosminsky and Rylance in season two of the hugely successful *Wolf Hall* for the BBC, where she played Dorothea, Cardinal Wolsey's daughter. She was widely praised for the climax of episode two, in an 'extraordinary scene' (*The Guardian*) between Dorothea (Khalique-Brown) and Thomas Cromwell (Mark Rylance).

Hannah can also be seen as Maggie Jones in the hit Netflix show *Black Doves* alongside Keira Knightley and Ben Whishaw, as well as opposite Staz Nair in the BBC1 crime drama *Virdee* and as series regular Sister Farouz in the hit HBO series *Dune Prophecy* opposite Emily Watson and Olivia Williams.

On the big screen Hannah had a memorable role opposite Margot Robbie and Kate McKinnon in the mega-hit film *Barbie*, written and directed by Greta Gerwig.

On stage, Hannah was the lead role in a brilliantly reviewed summer-long run of *The Secret Garden* at the Regent's Park Open Air Theatre for director Anna Himali Howard, receiving 5 stars from The Stage, The i Paper and more in 2024. Hannah previously starred as the lead in *I Know, I Know, I Know* at Southwark Playhouse.

When she's not acting, Hannah sings in the band Big Sky Orchestra.

Karim Khan – Writer

Karim Khan is a playwright and screenwriter based in Oxford. His sell-out show *Brown Boys Swim* won both the Fringe First and Popcorn Award at the Edinburgh Fringe 2022, and garnered a number of 5* and 4* before transferring to Soho Theatre for two runs and a national tour the following year. His play *Sweetmeats* will premiere at the Bush Theatre in 2026 in a co-production with Tara Theatre. He is currently working on new plays with the Royal Court Theatre, National Theatre and Soho Theatre. For screen, Karim wrote two episodes of *All Creatures Great and Small*, for which he won the Best Debut at the Edinburgh

TV Festival in 2023. He has been developing a number of original TV projects and has been in a number of writers rooms. He is currently directing his debut short film with the Amazon Prime and National Film and Television School. Karim graduated from there in 2019 on the MA Screenwriting programme. He has also been on the Soho Writers Lab and Royal Court Writers Group.

Adam Karim – Director

Adam's JMK Award-winning production of *Guards at the Taj* (Orange Tree Theatre) was nominated for a Stage Debut Award and won the Eastern Eye Best Director Award in 2025. He was previously Resident Director at the National Theatre Studio and Resident Assistant Director at the Donmar Warehouse.

Directing credits include: *Julius Caesar* (RADA), *Macbeth* (LAMDA), *Guards at the Taj* (Orange Tree Theatre), *MANTELPEACE* (Young Vic Taking Part), *Platform* (East15), Pressure Drop (Immediate Theatre / The Yard Theatre / schools tour), *Second Person Narrative* (Rose Bruford @ Omnibus Theatre).

Associate and Assistant Director credits include *Clyde's*, *When Winston Went To War With The Wireless*, *Trouble in Butetown* (Donmar Warehouse); *The P Word* (Bush Theatre, Olivier Award for Outstanding Achievement in Affiliate Theatre); *Sorry, You're Not A Winner* (Paines Plough).

Maariyah Sharjil – Set and Costume Designer

Maariyah's recent credits include: Designer for *Fy Enw i yw Rachel Corrie* (Theatr Cymru), *Vitamin D* (Soho Theatre), *Duck* (Arcola Theatre); Assistant Designer for *A Tupperware of Ashes* (National Theatre), *The Empress* (RSC), *Hakawatis* (Shakespeare's Globe); Assistant Costume Designer for *The Father and the Assassin* (National Theatre); Associate Designer for *Lavender, Hyacinth, Violet, Yew* (Bush Theatre), *As You Like It* (Shakespeare's Globe); Costume Researcher for *Life of Pi*

(American Repertory Theatre); and Costume Designer for *The Key Workers' Cycle* (Almeida Theatre). She is a first-class graduate from BA Design for Performance at the Royal Central School of Speech and Drama (2021). Before her design training, Maariyah worked at Sands Films as a costume constructor.

Holly Ellis – Lighting Designer

Holly Ellis is a graduate of LAMDA's technical theatre course.

Lighting Designer credits include: *Personal Values* (Hampstead Theatre); *Double Act* (Southwark Playhouse); *Bright Places*, *The Promise* (Birmingham Rep/UK Tour); *The Barber of Seville* (Waterperry Opera); *I'm Gonna Marry You Tobey Maguire*, *Blanket Ban* (Southwark Playhouse); *Errol's Garden* (UK Tour); *The Long Run* (New Diorama Theatre/ UK Tour); *Spy for Spy* (Riverside Studios); *On The Ropes* (Park Theatre); *Casteing* (Roundabout); *Animal Kingdom* (Hampstead Theatre Downstairs) and *Instructions for a Teenage Armageddon* (Southwark Playhouse – OffWestEnd Nomination for Best Lighting Design).

Associate Lighting Designer credits include: *Shanghai Dolls* (Kiln Theatre for Aideen Malone); *Kyoto* (@sohoplace for Aideen Malone); *A Sherlock Carol* (Marylebone Theatre for Rui Rita) and *Jabala and the Jinn* (Belgrade Theatre for Aideen Malone).

XANA – Composer and Sound Designer

XANA is a composer, spatial sound artist, music supervisor, musical director and a haptic specialist sound designer developing accessible audio systems for theatre and live art spaces. XANA is the recipient of the 2023 and 2024 Black British Theatre Awards for Best Sound Design and a nominee for Best Musical Direction on *Alterations* at the Black British Theatre Awards 2025; and the music science and technology lead and project mentor supporting Black artists and inventors at audio research label Inventing Waves.

Theatre credits: *After Sunday* (Belgrade Theatre); *Alterations* (National Theatre); *Shifters*, *Barcelona* (West End, Duke of York's); *Not Your Superwoman*, *Make Me Feel*, *The Real Ones*, *My Father's Fable*, *Elephant*, *Sleepova* (Offie nomination, Production Olivier Award), *The P Word* (Offie nomination, Production Olivier Award) and *Strange Fruit* at the Bush; *Pig Heart Boy* (Unicorn Theatre, UK Tour); *The Architect* (Actors Touring Company); *Beautiful Thing* (Stratford East); *Imposter 22*, *Word-Play* and *Living Newspaper #4* (Royal Court); *Rumble In the Jungle* (Rematch Live); *Anna Karenina* (Edinburgh Lyceum and Bristol Old Vic); *Intimate Apparel*, *The Trials* and *Marys Seacole* (Donmar Warehouse); *Earthworks*, *Sundown Kiki: Reloaded*, *The Collaboration*, *Sundown Kiki*, *Changing Destiny*, *Fairview* and *Ivan and the Dogs* (Young Vic); *...cake* (Theatre Peckham); *Burgerz* (Hackney Showroom); *King Troll [The Fawn]* (Offie nomination) and Deafinitely's *Everyday* (New Diorama); *Black Holes* (The Place, London); *Hive City Legacy* (Roundhouse); *Main Character Energy*, *But Daddy I Love Her*, *Glamrou: From Quran to Queen*, *Curious* and *Half-Breed* at Soho Theatre; *Blood Knot* and *Guards at the Taj* at the Orange Tree (both Offie nominations); *Samuel Takes a Break* and *SEX SEX MEN MEN* (Yard Theatre), *Is Dat Yu Yeah*, *Everything I Own* (Brixton House). Music includes featuring in the song 'Afronaut' on Seed Ensemble's album, *Driftglass* (Mercury Prize nomination).

Rakhee Sharma – Movement Director

Rakhee Sharma is a multidisciplinary artist with a unique approach to movement, shaped by her neurodiverse perspective. Her work is influenced by somatic dance, Indian philosophy, and physical theatre. Rakhee began her career as a dancer and choreographer in the Bollywood film industry before training as an actor at the Royal Central

School of Speech and Drama, where she received the prestigious Lawrence Olivier Bursary Award.

Recent theatre includes: *Marriage Material* (Associate) (Lyric Theatre); *Santi and Naz* (Soho Theatre / UK Tour); *Macbeth* (Guildhall); *Silence* (Donmar Warehouse); *Bitter-Enders* (Arcola Theatre); *The Walden* (Associate) (Harold Pinter Theatre); *Sparks, Red Velvet, The Christians* (LAMDA).

Recent film and television includes: *Wild Cherry* (Associate Movement Director) (BBC); *Incompatible* (BFI Short).

Gurnesha Bola – Dramaturg

Gurnesha is a freelance dramaturg, reader and programmer. She reads for both subsidised and commercial theatre companies as well as major playwriting prizes including the Bruntwood Prize and the Theatre503 International Playwriting Award. She is currently working as a dramaturg on plays commissioned by Hampstead Theatre, Bush Theatre and the Old Fire Station. Gurnesha was previously Literary Associate at the Royal Court.

Gurkiran Kaur – Dialect Coach

Recent theatre credits: *Elmet* (The Javaad Alipoor Company); *I'll Burn The Ocean/For You* (Talawa Theatre Company); *Come Fall in Love* (Playful Productions); *Millennium Girls* (Brixton House); *The Da Vinci Code* (Wiltshire Creative); *Sophia* (Eastern Angles Theatre); *Bangers* (SH Productions); *Ghost Stories* (HighTide); *King Troll* (Kali Theatre & New Diorama); *A Tupperware of Ashes* (National Theatre); *Peanut Butter & Blueberries* (Kiln Theatre); *Dylan Mulvaney: FAGHAG* (Soho Theatre); *Refugee!* (62 Gladstone Street); *The Secret Garden* (Regent's Park Open Air Theatre); *Expendable, Dugsi Dayz* (Royal Court); *Red Pitch* (@sohoplace); *Sweat, Great Expectations* (Royal Exchange), *The Buddha of Suburbia, Falkland Sounds, The Empress* (Royal Shakespeare Company), *blackbird hour..., Wolves On Road, The Real Ones, The Cord, A Playlist for the Revolution, Paradise Now,*

The P Word, Favour, Red Pitch (Bush Theatre); *This Much I Know, Lotus Beauty* (Hampstead Theatre); *The Enormous Crocodile: The Musical* (Leeds Playhouse).

TV & film credits: *Good Karma Hospital* (ITV & Tiger Aspect Productions); *Hotel Portofino* (ITV, PBS & Eagle Eye); *Strange Evidence* (Matt's Gallery).

Jessie Anand – Producer

Jessie is a theatre and opera producer working across the UK and internationally. Her productions include recent Bush Theatre hits *Tender* and *This Might Not Be It*; Untapped Award-winning show *The Mosinee Project*, which sold out its Edinburgh Fringe run in 2024; Offie Award-winning productions *Yellowfin* and *The Bleeding Tree* at Southwark Playhouse; and Virginia Woolf-inspired solo show *Orlando*, which transferred to New York as part of Brits Off Broadway. She works as an in-house producer at Jermyn Street Theatre and she is the company producer for Airlock Theatre, with whom she has premiered *Count Dykula* (Soho Theatre / regional tour) and *Pansexual Pregnant Piracy* (Soho Theatre). She has also worked with and for companies including the National Theatre, Belarus Free Theatre, Wayward Productions, Kandinsky, Oxford Opera and The Big House. Jessie is supported by new producers' charity Stage One.

Dan Knight – Production Manager

Dan trained as a musician, specializing in composition for the screen and has composing and sound design credits on several short films and an original musical. He also has Musical Directorship credits for *The Wedding Singer*, and *The Addams Family* (Oxford Playhouse), as well as having performed in the pit on a number of productions as a drummer and percussionist (*Oliver, Legally Blonde, Chicago, 9 to 5*).

The crossover between music and the stage eventually led him towards the murky depths of backstage theatre and after completing a Masters in Post-16 education, he taught backstage theatre production on Abingdon & Witney College's Performing Arts course for six years. Several of his students now hold positions in the West End and many continue to work in Oxford's own theatre district. Dan joined the OFS in 2024 and now oversees technical operations for both in house and visiting productions.

Olivia Wolfenden – Stage Manager

Olivia trained at LAMDA.

Her professional credits include: *Measure For Measure* (LAMDA); *[BLANK]* (LAMDA); *Cinderella* (The Hexagon); *Macbeth* (LAMDA); *Persephone* (Little Angel Theatre); *She Loves Me* (Mountview)*; Sleeping Beauty* (The Hexagon; Panto Awards Nominee 2024)*; The Island* (Archway Hospital); *Primary Playwrights* (Soho Theatre); *Under The Kundè Tree* (Southwark Playhouse Borough; Offies Nominee, British Black Theatre Awards Nominee); *The Walworth Farce* (Southwark Playhouse Elephant); *Jack and the Beanstalk* (The Hexagon; Panto Awards Nominee 2023); *Mary* (Hampstead Theatre); *Get Dressed!* (The Unicorn); *Divine* (ArtsEd); *Pericles* (Jackson's Lane); *Beauty and the Beast* (The Hexagon; Panto Awards Winner 2022)*; It's Beautiful Over There* (Tristan Bates Theatre); *Last Easter* (Orange Tree Theatre); *Cinderella* (The Hexagon; Panto Awards Nominee 2020); *Handbagged* (Salisbury Playhouse); *I'm Sorry But* (Bread and Roses); Pride in London 2019.

A note from the Old Fire Station

The Old Fire Station is a hopeful, human-friendly place for people to be, think and create. In the fourteen years since we first opened our doors, we have become a popular and thriving multi-form arts centre and an incubator for place-based change, anchored in community. We support and train partners locally and nationally to use 'Storytelling', an approach to impact measurement that centres the voices of people at the heart of a piece of work. What makes us a bit unusual is that we share our building and a deep partnership with the homelessness charity Crisis. This enables us to include people who are homeless or vulnerably housed in everything we do. We run our cafe with Damascus Rose Kitchen, a social enterprise by and for refugee women, working together to offer a welcoming place that brings together people from all walks of life.

Imagination – the capacity to conceive of what doesn't yet exist – is the engine of social and individual change, and art and creativity are where imaginations flourish. Therefore, we believe it is critical that everyone can participate in making and sharing art and are concerned with how to make this a reality.

These aren't easy times to make new plays, but with intensifying polarization and widening social divides, it's more urgent than ever that we share stories that represent a diversity of lived experiences, to continue to do what theatre does so extraordinarily well – nurturing empathy, understanding and connection through story, while also challenging us to imagine and understand the world beyond our own perspectives and experiences.

More than anything, this is a time that requires the active and muscular nurturing of hope – not as a passive emotion, but as an ethical stance that insists on imagining a better world and believes in the possibility of social justice. Art – an act of creativity, strengthens our capacity for hope. To make art, we must step into a space of unknowing, we must trust the process, we must manifest something that previously didn't exist in the world and we must imagine that it matters to do so.

Karim and the rest of the team have done just that with this remarkable new play, and we are very proud to have been able to play a part in its becoming.

The Old Fire Station team

Andrew Jones, Box-Office Coordinator

Becca Vallins, Deputy CEO

Bethan Elford, Exhibitions and Workshops Manager

Caroline Richmond, Finance Manager

Clara Vaughan, CEO

Chris Michael, Bookings and Administration Manager

Dan Knight, Technical Manager

Darran Ijada, Storytelling Administrator

Emma Joynson, Office Administrator

Hebe York, Cafe Manager

Jak Soroka, Front of House Assistant

Leila Al-Hassan, Fundraising Officer

Liza Roure, Head of Fundraising

Lizzie McHale, Front of House Coordinator

Megan Dawkins, Head of HR and Operations

Molly Davies, Marketing Manager

Rebecca Morris, Head of Programming

Sarah Cassidy, Head of Engagement and Learning

Sasa Cheung, Bookkeeper

Special thanks to Arts Council England, PF Charitable Trust and Howes Percival LLP for supporting *Before the Millennium,* alongside many generous individual donations.

Before the Millennium

My creative journey began at the age of eight when I went to a Sunday drama class, and on my very first day I auditioned to be in a Christmas show at the Old Fire Station. The show was *Snow White and the Seven Dwarves* and the role I went on to land was Sleepy. Many have said it was a rousing performance, and of course I went full method. Twenty-three years later, I'm returning to the OFS with my own Christmas show. As a writer, there's stories you create and yearn to get made for years and years, endlessly confronting hurdles and curve balls that come your way. TV development has taught me that the hard way. The truth is I never envisaged writing a Christmas show, or that I'd have another play in Oxford after *Brown Boys Swim*. I'm truly grateful to have received this opportunity. It's taught me to be open to the universe's offerings, and to not hold so tightly to the things I think I want, because sometimes something even better might be around the corner to surprise you.

Perhaps I thought I wasn't 'allowed' to write a Christmas show. For as long as I can remember, I've been asked the question 'do you celebrate Christmas?'. It's almost as common as the question 'not even water?' during Ramadan. And of course, in 1999 Christmas and Ramadan overlapped in such a beautifully synchronous way. But, as Pakistanis and Muslims, we do partake in Christmas, whether it's intentional or not – we fundamentally contribute to what makes it what it is, and in *Before the Millennium* you'll witness Christmas through our prism.

Media and politicians will continue to scapegoat and vilify migrants and asylum seekers to distract us from the more insidious things at hand, like wealth inequality, austerity and using tax-payer money to fund a genocide against Palestinians – all while said migrants treat their relatives in hospitals and are at the front line of every public service. This country would fall on its knees if it wasn't for our migrants, and yet, I truly believe we needn't do anything to seek approval, acceptance or validation from those who struggle to see our humanity; that's their problem to work through.

With *Before the Millennium*, I wanted to centre the experiences of migrant women who have sacrificed so much as they've transplanted their lives here. I wouldn't be here if it wasn't for them. As children of the diaspora, we feel every sacrifice our parents have made, and yet we remain helpless in recognising the truism that nothing we do can quite repay what they have done for us. In writing this play, I want to honour and celebrate them, but most importantly make them feel seen.

KK.

My heartfelt thanks to:

Amaani Khan. Maryam Mir. Waleed Akhtar. Mike Bartlett. Aqsa Altaff. Saeed Khan. Kelly Knatchbull.

Adam Karim. Jessie Anand. Gurnesha Bola. Clara Vaughan. Molly Davies.

Hannah Khalique-Brown. Gurjot Dhaliwal. Prabhleen Oberoi.

The creative team. The Old Fire Station.

x.

For Mumma

Notes.

This is a two act play with an interval in between. This play should feel dreamy and ethereal and capture the essence of the end of the 1990s, and the cusp of the millennium, seeped with a healthy dose of Woolworths nostalgia. Most of the play will take place in the Woolies Cowley store unless they're in the freezing cold outside. This play should flow and hold a rhythm.

Urdu/Punjabi lines are written phonetically.

– suggests interruption.

/ suggests overlapping dialogue.

Act One

One

We're in **1999**. *We're in* **Woolworths**. *It's bright and colourful – that's just the pick n mix section. There's a touch of magic about this place. Christmas gifts are stacked on shelves. The place is adorned with tinsel, shiny decoration. '90s Christmas music plays. Mood party lighting. We're at their Christmas staff party.*

Zoya *and* **Iqra** (*both 26, Pakistani*) *face one another, paper cups in hand. They are wearing paper party hats and Woolworths uniform, but with a smatter of glitter and sparkle. The pair watch the shenanigans around them, entertained.*

Zoya   He said 'do you celebrate Christmas?'

Iqra   Kya?

Zoya (*louder this time*)   Do you celebrate Christmas?

Zoya *points him out.* **Iqra** *tries to look who it is –*

Iqra   Kaun? Baldy or fatty?

Zoya   Iqra!

Iqra   Stop spitting in my ear, kutti.

Zoya (*touching* **Iqra**'s *earlobe playfully*)   Kaan kholo. Mr Edwards, Woolies ka branch manager.

Iqra   Achaa! Fatty . . . what did you say in reply?

Zoya   I said hanji, Merry Christmas Mr Edwards. To you and yours. I hope the new millennium brings you nothing but good things.

Iqra *just watches her, disturbed –*

Zoya   Kya? this is what people say.

Iqra   Did you tell him your husband works the whole Christmas day? (*Mocking.*) 'To you and yours'.

Zoya   We don't all have papa ka fortune, Lahori girl. Some of us need money.

Iqra   Is there sharab in that cup?

Iqra *takes it, sips it.*

Iqra   Fikar nahi kar, you will make it back to Pakistan.

Zoya   Inshallah –

Iqra   You can take some of my shifts –

Zoya   Nahi – just don't stop doing your duas for me.

Iqra   These nights they multiply –

Zoya   Christmas?

Iqra   Nahi Ramzan. The gorray have radicalised you. The only thing we should be celebrating is Quad-e-Azam, not Jesus Christ.

Zoya   Astaghfrullah. Jesus is our prophet too. Eesa alai-his salam.

Iqra   But he wasn't born December twenty-fifth, like humaaray founding father. I would ban Christmas in Pakistan.

Zoya   Achaa? Prime Minister Scrooge saab.

Iqra   Whoever celebrates it pays an additional 2% tax. Oi, yeh dekho. Didn't his wife leave him two months ago?

Zoya   Nahi, three months hogai.

Iqra   Hahn, acha, now look. He's trying his luck with her. Beth.

Zoya   Nahi, not Beth –

Iqra   Hai meri Allah –

Zoya   It's the sharab, this isn't him –

Iqra   Look how uninhibited he is, he's so . . . alive.

Zoya   Unin-kya?

Iqra   Uninhibited. (*Gestures letters on* **Zoya**'s *palm*.)   U n i n
h i b i t e d.

Zoya   Iska matlab kya hai?

Iqra   Not controlled or restrained. Free to say or feel
whatever's deep inside –

Zoya   Nahi, he doesn't look free, he looks . . . sad.

Iqra   I would enforce a rehabilitation programme for all
heartbroken men before they re-enter society. My Christmas
tax would fund it.

Zoya   Poor man, we should help him –

Iqra *stops* **Zoya** *from intervening.*

Iqra   Don't you watch those Christmas movies? What's the
one thing everyone wants for Christmas? . . . Pyar.
Mohabbat. Love, Zoya.

Zoya   *'All I Want for Christmas Is You'.*

Iqra   Hahn ji, it's the end of the year, no worse – one entire
millennium, who knows what happens next, where we end
up, we could lose everything –

Zoya   Tauba karru. Don't say that.

Iqra   That's what they're saying. And the end of anything
will always feel like the end of life, like time will just stop for
him, all of us – and the thought that he'd leave this dunya all
alone is . . . too sad for him to bear, that he'll even try his
luck at a Woolies staff party . . . with Beth.

Zoya   Aw, fikar nahi kar. I'll find you a good sharif boy to
keep you company in the 2000s.

Iqra   I'm not talking about me, kutti –

Zoya   You never saw my wedding. The world would have to end for me to not see yours – I will dance at your shaadi til my feet grow chaalay.

Iqra   That's disgusting, Zoya.

Zoya (*hugs her*)   I'll find a sona larka just as smart as you. Your First Gentleman.

Iqra   That's impossible –

Zoya   With soni moonchey, and velvet suits and bow ties –

Iqra   Does your husband know you fantasize about this man?

Zoya   I wonder if I'm what he expected?

Iqra   Yeh kya bakwaas?

Zoya   We were just given each other, me and him. He didn't choose me, and if he could –

Iqra   Zoya, chupp! What did I say? Don't let those thoughts ever enter your head. He's thanking Allah in every dua to be blessed with a woman as beautiful as you.

Zoya's *heart melts, she smiles at* **Iqra**. **Iqra** *notices something.*

Zoya   How have you not found an Oxford waala? Three years in Brasenose and still kuche beh nahi?

Iqra   Pakistani boys confound me . . . look at Musharaf and Sharif – corrupt as each other.

Zoya   Come on yaar, we all know you'll end up with a chittah safed gora. Will you show it to me when you graduate? –

Iqra   Kya?

Zoya   Brasenose.

Iqra   Of course. (*Uneasy.*)

Zoya   I'll tell ammi and abbu I was right there, inside Oxford.

Iqra   You're already in Oxford.

Zoya   Add it to the list. (*Removes purse.*)

Iqra   Right now? –

Zoya   It needs to be written for it happen.

Zoya *passes it to her and then a pen.* **Iqra** *reluctantly takes it. And then gets* **Zoya**'s *back and writes on it.* **Zoya** *giggles.*

Iqra   Hold still. I can take you there anytime. It's pretty with the Christmas tree.

Zoya   Nahi I'll see it when you graduate. Is Millennium Dome there too?

Iqra   Kya?

Zoya   On the list? Did you write it?

Iqra   Nahi.

Zoya *shuffles, shocked.* **Iqra** *notices something.*

Zoya   Add it then.

Iqra   Oi, yeh dekho.

Zoya   Kya?

Iqra (*gestures discreetly*)   She's been staring at us.

Suddenly we see her, but maybe only her back. A South Asian woman in her twenties just like them.

Zoya   Let me talk to her . . . she might be lost.

Iqra   Nahi Zoya – if she wants to talk to us, she'll come to us, now I want to dance. Mujhe yeh gana pasand hai.

Iqra *takes* **Zoya**'s *hand and starts dancing.* **Zoya** *struggles to get into it, and then she does.*

Zoya   Since when have you danced?

Iqra   I don't trust 2000. It feels wrong.

Zoya   Are you scared? Oh my god. You are!

Iqra   Power grids, transport systems, communication networks could all be disrupted – nuclear weapons could go off –

Zoya *isn't listening, she can't stop watching her.* **Zoya** *waves at her, gesturing for her to come over.*

Iqra   What you doing? Stop that, Zoya. (*Shouting out.*) Woolies band hai – closed. Opening hours 9am til 8pm.

Zoya   Except bank holidays and special occasions.

Iqra   Hahnji, except bank holidays –

Zoya (*to girl*)   Idar ao. Come here! She won't bite. (*To* **Iqra**.) You're scaring her.

A beat. The girl comes towards them, a bit dazed, stunned.

Zoya   She's wearing uniform.

(*To girl.*) Kya tumhay meree samajh aa rahee hai? Maybe she speaks Pashto or Bihari.

Iqra (*like she's talking to someone deaf, and in English*)   What are you doing here?

Zoya   Iqra! Stop being rude.

Faiza   I work here. Hi.

They're both stunned. She's got an English accent.

Iqra (*disgusted*)   Since when?

Faiza   I'm doing the holiday shifts. Temping. But I'm starting properly tomorrow. Nice to meet you. I'm Faiza.

Zoya   She's a student like you!

Faiza   No, I'm not actually –

Iqra   I've never seen you around.

Zoya   Oxford, or Oxford Brookes?

Faiza   Neither / which do you go.

Iqra   Where do you go?

Faiza   I never went uni.

Iqra   Kya? –

Zoya   Why are you nosy. (*To* **Faiza**.) I'm sorry about my friend–

Faiza   No it's okay. I wanted to go Glasgow –

Zoya   Glasgow? –

Faiza   Glasgow School of Art which / is a bit far.

Iqra   She's an artist! –

Zoya   Are you an artist? –

Faiza   Kind of.

Zoya   Shaabash, that's impressive –

Faiza   / Thank you.

Iqra   Why didn't you go Glasgow? –

Zoya   Stop it, you're doing it again –

Faiza   No it's okay. My mum didn't want me moving away.

Iqra   Zoya, British Pakistani are fascinating specimen.

Faiza   Zoya? You're Zoya?

Zoya   Yes.

Faiza *can't believe her eyes.* **Zoya** *and* **Iqra** *stare at each other. Confused.*

Zoya   Kya?

Faiza   Nothing!

Iqra   What did she say?

Zoya   Do you know me?

Faiza   No –

Iqra   You know this girl?!

Zoya   Nahi, I don't think so?

Iqra (*to* **Faiza**)   Who's been talking to you about her? Iskee sass? Mother-in-law, sister-in-law? Postman? Who do you know? –

Zoya   Stop it, you're scaring her–

Faiza   No, it's okay.

Zoya   Are you okay?

Faiza   You're . . . beautiful.

Zoya   Aw, thank you, aw that's nice, isn't it. (*Turning to* **Iqra**.)

Iqra   Zoya is not a lesbian. Show her your husband's photo–

Faiza   I didn't mean it like that –

Zoya   She's paying me a compliment! You cut her off. Aur batao. (*enjoying it*)

Iqra   Where you from? –

Faiza   Here. Oxford –

Iqra   Yahan se? Pakistani? –

Faiza   Yes / what about you?

Iqra   Kahaan se? –

Faiza   Erm . . . Lahore –

Zoya (*to* **Iqra**)   Iqra's from Lahore –

Iqra   Which part?

Faiza   Erm y'know the old side.

Iqra   Old side? Achaa. (*smirks*)

Zoya   You've never been?

Iqra   Look at these desi-born goray – they can't even point where they're from on a map, I will not raise my children here, BBCD, that's what they are –

Zoya (*to* **Iqra**)   Then where will you raise them? –

Faiza   B b c d?

Iqra   British-born confused desi – look at what's she's wearing. How did we let these fools colonise us?

Zoya   Chup-nee, she's an artist!

Faiza (*to* **Zoya**)   Where are you from?

Zoya   Rawalpindi. I came here after I got married –

Iqra   To Jamal. He was born here . . . like you.

Faiza (*to* **Zoya**)   Are you happy? –

Zoya   What?

Faiza   Sorry ignore me.

Zoya   Yes . . . of course, why?

Faiza   It must've been a big shift for you, coming here –

Zoya   Iqra goes to Oxford. She studies Politics. Nahi, *reads* Politics.

Iqra   Kutti, why are you sharing my details?

Zoya   What you worried for? In years to come, everyone will know Iqra Razwan because she will be the first woman Prime Minister –

Iqra   Benazir be tee –

Zoya   Second woman Prime Minister of Pakistan –

Iqra   Inshallah. One day maybe.

Zoya   Before that she'll work right here for the MP's office in Mr Blair ka government next year. Tell her about your job –

Iqra   Are you gonna tell her the last time I did a tatti too?

Zoya   She wants – kya nam tah–

Iqra   Reparations, Zoya! –

Zoya   She wants reparations from the Brits for what was done –

Faiza   That feels like a great idea –

Iqra   See! Shukria bahut.

Zoya   It's your country she's talking about!

Faiza   I don't endorse this country –

Zoya   You can't say that!

Iqra   Why not? –

Faiza   I didn't think you'd be like this.

Iqra   Like what?

Zoya   Araam-se –

Faiza   It doesn't matter –

Iqra (*to* **Zoya**)   She knows me as well –

Faiza   I don't –

Iqra   What do you know of me? –

Faiza   Nothing –

Iqra   Have you been circulating my pictures? (*Turns to* **Zoya**.) Trying to get me a rishta. What did I say? I'm not made for the shackles of marriage –

Faiza   It's not like that.

Zoya   Meh na kya kiah? I've done nothing.

Faiza   I can confirm that no rishta pics have made their way to me.

Zoya   You're being paranoid Iqra.

Iqra   Who taught you that word? Huh? I taught you that word. Paranoid!

Zoya   I like her. Welcome to Woolies, Faiza.

Faiza *smiles.* **Iqra** *gasps in disbelief.*

Two

Iqra *is poring through papers, stressed and anxious, while* **Zoya** *holds a snow globe. She shakes it and stares at it. It's empty. She marvels at it.*

Zoya   There's no snow.

Iqra   Kya?

Zoya   They didn't fill it with snow. We can't sell this.

Iqra   Idar doh.

Iqra *abruptly picks it up and shakes it.*

Zoya   I'll report it.

Iqra *drops it.* **Zoya** *catches it before it smashes to the ground. She's shocked.*

Zoya   You're lucky Jamal taught me how to play cricket. Kee hoya?

Iqra *is stressed, returns looking through papers. She shuffles her Dawn newspaper, concealing something.*

Iqra   Kuch bhee nahi.

Zoya   The military rule will end inshallah! (*Acknowledging paper.*)

Iqra   Sharif was no angel. The whole system needs reform.

Zoya   Stop reading the news, okay.

Iqra   Chor'na. it's not even about that.

Zoya   Kya baht hai? Is it your professor? What marks did you get?

A beat.

Iqra   Why does it even matter? Nothing I do will ever mean anything.

Zoya   Don't say that!

Zoya *is about to comfort* **Iqra** *when* **Faiza** *appears –*

Faiza   Sorry. I didn't mean to interrupt.

Zoya   You didn't. I need to show you around.

Faiza   Yes please. I'd love to have a look around the place.

Zoya (*to* **Iqra**)   Tum bhi ao, uhtt.

Zoya *watches* **Iqra** *who stays still.* **Iqra** *watches them, concerned –*

Iqra   You don't need me.

Zoya   You were here first.

A beat. **Iqra** *doesn't move.*

Faiza   Is that what happened? how did you start working here?

Zoya   Iqra got me the job. No one would take a woman who couldn't read or write. We pretended.

Faiza   What do you mean, 'pretended'?

Zoya   Every day, every shift, she'd teach me a little, so we didn't have to pretend anymore –

Faiza   That's so sweet of her.

Zoya   She'll soften to you. Like rusk to chai. (*Suddenly worried.*) You won't tell anyone, will you?

Iqra   She wouldn't dare –

Faiza   Of course I wouldn't.

Zoya Because I can read and write now. (*Reads something off the wall.*)

Faiza No of course, you can trust me.

Iqra Can we?

Faiza I won't tell anyone I promise.

Iqra (*to* **Faiza**) How did *you* get this job?

A beat.

Faiza I applied –

Iqra How? –

Faiza The same way you did! –

Zoya (*to* **Iqra**) Are you part of my tour or not? (*A beat.*) Then chupp!

Iqra *sits and reads some papers, watching the pair, concerned for* **Zoya**.

Zoya The pick n mix stall needs to be refilled regularly. The cola bottles and fudge are the popular ones, the bachey love them, but anything that looks low needs to be refilled immediately. They need to look like they're bursting, like this –

Zoya *refills them. She takes moments to glance at* **Iqra**, *almost suspicious of what he's up to.*

Zoya Now you try.

Faiza *copies her.*

Faiza Am I doing it right?

Zoya Shaabash. You're a natural.

Faiza D'you think?

Zoya Yes! Of course.

Faiza Thank you!

Iqra   It's not quantum physics is it?

Zoya   Then why don't you ever do it?

Iqra   I have other things to do –

Zoya   Of course you do. Kya karahe ho? (*Glancing at her papers.*)

Iqra *moves it away. A beat.*

Zoya   What do you think of the Santa display? I did that all by myself.

Iqra   I had a paper to hand in, a 9am lecture –

Zoya   Give me your artist opinion, Faiza.

Faiza   It's beautiful. I love the wintry trees, the way the presents are piled up high –

Zoya   But something doesn't look right – I can't put my finger on it, can you see?

The pair look at it. For a moment they almost mirror each other organically. **Iqra** *notices this, takes this in.*

Faiza   No, it looks . . . perfect.

Iqra   Why you lying for?

Faiza   I'm not! –

Iqra   What isn't wrong with it –

Faiza   No, you can tell a lot of care's gone into it –

Iqra (*to* **Zoya**)   Kia chah tee hai humse?

Faiza   I can understand y'know.

Iqra   I should hope so.

Zoya (*to* **Iqra**)   Just because your mum isn't here doesn't mean you forget the manners she brought you up with.

Faiza   I don't want anything from you, Iqra. Genuinely.

Zoya   Ignore her, all she wants is attention!

Iqra   Why can't you see it, Zoya? –

Zoya   It will need a wipe from time to time – dust shust. The floors will need mopping too, at the end of every day. You rinse then squeeze, so the water doesn't splatter across it. (*For* **Iqra**.) There's a rota on the door, same for toilets.

Faiza   Okay.

Zoya   And remember people come here to bring their loved ones gifts – it's your job to make it special. Smile, talk to children, ask them questions, offer help, 'is there anything else I can help with sir? Have a lovely day. Merry Christmas'.

Iqra   Ugh –

Zoya   She'll be fine once she's filled her peht.

Iqra   No one loves Woolworths as much as humaaray pyari Zoya –

Zoya   It's been good to both of us – even though you don't know how to show it back.

Iqra   I treat it like a job that pays me – it's what everyone does.

Zoya   Of course, behn ji here has bigger fish to fry. Woolies is beneath her.

Iqra   No it's not –

Faiza (*to* **Zoya**)   It means more to you?

Zoya   I don't have the problem of Pakistan to solve, do I? Or Kashmir.

Iqra   Why do you taunt me for having any ambition?

Zoya   Because I don't have any of it, that's why!

Iqra   Zoya, don't be like this!

Zoya   Nahi, if I was as smart as you, I might be the same –

Iqra   You are, Zoya, sharper than me. Who could learn English in months?

Zoya   Chorro! this is all I'm good for.

Faiza   Nahi, why won't you just (*catches herself*)

Zoya   What? –

Faiza   Nothing –

Iqra   I can't stand this – (*Referring to music.*)

Zoya   What's wrong with it?

Iqra   This is what hell will be like. The same five songs on loop. Faiza? Every girl who starts here, must leave their mark somehow.

Zoya   Nahi, Iqra.

Faiza   What is it?

Iqra   Will you do something for me?

Zoya   / Ignore her Faiza.

Faiza   What? –

Zoya   She wants to play desi music on the shop stereo. I can't lose this job, Iqra.

Iqra   You won't. If we get into trouble, I'll take full blame.

Zoya   Araam kar. She doesn't know how to relax.

Faiza   Why is it so important? –

Iqra   Why won't you let me fulfil my single wish? Just once. Then I'll stop.

Zoya   There's customers here!

Iqra   They'll enjoy it.

Zoya   Woolies isn't for bhangra gaana shaana, people want Christmas music, people want Cliff Richard –

Iqra   Fuck Cliff Richard –

(*To* **Faiza**.) Here you go.

Iqra *passes her the cassette.* **Faiza** *watches it.*

Iqra   Go on! What you waiting for?

Zoya   Faiza give it to me please.

Faiza *doesn't know what to do, torn between the women.*

Faiza   Where is it?

Iqra   At the back in the store room –

Faiza   I don't know how it works –

Iqra   It's a bloody stereo, Faiza!

Zoya   You'll get yourself fired. Us too. Is that what you want? I won't touch you because I don't know you, I've only just met you, so I'll reason with you, woman to woman, colleague to colleague, Faiza, please: chorro. (*Something in* **Zoya***'s tone feels different.* **Faiza** *notices.*)

A beat. Something about this triggers **Faiza** *viscerally. The space distorts into a snow globe. The moment is suspended, as* **Iqra** *and* **Zoya** *remain still, frozen. Only* **Faiza** *can move.*

Faiza *moves closer, about to touch her, when the moment returns to the shop, the present.* **Faiza** *passes* **Zoya** *the tape.* **Zoya** *clasps it with relief.* **Faiza** *leaves.*

Zoya   Where are you going?

The pair watch her go. A beat.

Iqra   You need to be careful around her, Zoya.

Zoya   Why are you trying to get rid of her?

Iqra   She's here for some reason and I don't know what it is, but I don't like it.

Zoya   She needs money. We all do. Well, not you.

Iqra   She has this intense obsession with you. It's unnerving.

Zoya *laughs.*

Iqra   Kya?

Zoya   You're jealous! Because bilkul everyone – without fail – falls in love with Iqra Razwan.

Iqra   Oh my god. We're doing this again?

Zoya   And the first time someone shows me the slightest bit of attention –

Iqra   Everyone gives you attention Zoya.

Zoya   Jhoot nahi bol. Who do I have? Siraf, you and Jamal.

Iqra   She could be part of his family. Have you considered that?

Zoya   Kya bakwaas? I've met his whole family.

Iqra   Have you? What if they sent someone to spy on you. What does bhabi do when she's not at home.

Zoya   Don't plant these thoughts in my head okay!

Iqra   I don't trust her.

Zoya   You don't trust anyone, Iqra. This is your problem. You never let anyone in, apart from Quad-e-Azam.

Iqra   Stop being facetious.

Zoya   Stop saying words I don't understand. Your first impressions are always wrong. Remember what you thought of me.

Iqra   I won't leave your sight when she's around, mein is se ziyaada nahi bollon gee.

Zoya   Kya baht hai? Why are you being so protective? Huh?

A beat. **Iqra** *evades the question.*

Three

The next day. The brink of sunset. **Zoya** *opens her flask and her Tupperware,* **Iqra** *looks inside. She's shocked to her core, smells it, thrilled.*

Iqra   You remembered?

Zoya   How could I forget? Jamal's at his ammi's, it was your turn.

Iqra   You're 'home alone'?

Zoya   Hahn – bilkul Kevin McCallister! Merry / Christmas, ya filthy animal!

Iqra   Christmas, ya filthy animal! Make the food that *you* like, Zoya. Humay bhool jao.

Zoya   What's the point in that?

Iqra   Some days you'll only have yourself to feed.

Zoya   Will that be your campaign ki slogan? feed yourself?

Iqra   Zoya you genius . . . (*Brainstorming.*) We must feed ourselves, it's high time, after years of Western meddling. Fuck the Amreekans, the English.

Zoya *looking around, calming her down and to see if* **Faiza** *is around.*

Zoya   What if she's here to replace me? –

Iqra   Nahi, that can't be . . . (*Processing.*)

Zoya   She's British with a British accent. She'll be an improvement –

Iqra   You're good at this, Zoya, they wouldn't do that. If they're replacing anyone, it's me.

Zoya   It could be both of us. She's temping here until Christmas, learning from us, the moment 2000 comes, they'll throw us out like garbage.

Iqra   Would that be such a bad thing?

Zoya   Kya?

Iqra   You want to go back.

Zoya   With what money? Where is she?

Iqra   What you doing?

Zoya   She should eat with us.

Iqra   There's only enough for two –

Zoya   Don't be greedy acha? I made extra –

Iqra   For your replacement? How charitable of you –

Zoya   Chupp (*calls out*) FAIZA!

Iqra *jumps.* **Faiza** *arrives almost instantly, freaking them out.*

Zoya   Do you have a roza?

Faiza *nods.*

Zoya   Then come eat with us, ao.

Faiza   No, it's okay –

Zoya   D'you have khaana shaana?

Faiza *shakes head.*

Zoya   Bett jao –

Faiza   Are you sure?

Zoya   Of course –

Iqra   Idor doh, kulgaya.

Zoya *passes the dates around. They each break their fast.* **Zoya** *does a dua, hands clasped together.* **Faiza** *too, staring at* **Zoya**. **Iqra** *just eats it.* **Zoya** *pours in the food–*

Zoya   Do you plan to stay here after Christmas?

Faiza   I'd love to –

Zoya   You would? –

Faiza   But I can't –

Iqra   Kyu?

Faiza   I'm . . . I'm going away for a bit . . .

Iqra   Where are / you going?

Faiza (*changing subject*)   That smells gorgeous.

Zoya   Do you like gobi?

Faiza   Yeah I do . . .

Iqra   Why are you hesitating?

Faiza   I didn't like it so much when I was growing up, but now I do.

Zoya   That was me with bhindian.

Iqra (*to* **Faiza**)   What's wrong with you?

Zoya   It's Iqra's favourite.

Faiza   Is that why you cooked it? –

Iqra   What's it to you?

Zoya   / Stop being rude!

Iqra   Mmm, Zoya, yeh boht zabardast hai.

Zoya (*to* **Faiza**)   What changed?

Faiza   I don't know. (*A beat.*) When I was little my mum would make it all the time, and I'd refuse it.

Zoya   How could you refuse your mother's cooking?

Iqra   Like a little British desi princess –

Zoya   A mother's cooking is gold –

Faiza (*amused*)   I don't know . . . I just didn't like it, not really – until one day I was so hungry, I'd never felt hunger like that, in the pit of my stomach –

Iqra   It was a roza?

Faiza   No, not even a roza, my body couldn't take anything, I felt so empty, until I go into the kitchen, open the fridge and I see it in this plastic box – the gobi she made. And it was the most . . . delicious thing I'd ever tasted.

Iqra   When you're hungry everything is good –

Zoya   Nahi ji, did you not hear her? Her body couldn't take anything – did you ever tell her?

Faiza   What?

Zoya   Your ammi? How much you liked it, that it was the most delicious thing you'd ever tasted.

Faiza *shakes her head.*

Zoya   The moment you go back home, you tell her.

A beat.

Faiza   I don't think I can.

Zoya   Kyu nahi?

A beat, **Faiza** *struggling with this.* **Zoya** *notices.*

Zoya   Are you okay?

Faiza   . . . we've stopped talking.

Zoya   Kya hua?

Iqra   Why you being nosy Zoya?

Zoya   Look who's talking. (*To* **Faiza**.) I'm sorry. Ignore me.

Faiza   No it's okay, it's just . . . I'm going away. She's finding that hard.

Iqra   Kahaan? Where you trotting off to?

Faiza   Alaska, it's this residency. I'll be working with the local community there –

Zoya   Alaska? Yeh Kahaan hai?

Iqra   Amreeka –

Zoya   That's far.

Faiza   I know, but I couldn't just miss this. It's what I've wanted to do for so long –

Iqra   What? To paint snow?

Faiza   Mountains and skies, the colour that streaks through them when the aurora borealis comes –

Zoya   How long will that take?

Faiza   I'll be there a year . . . But it could be longer.

Zoya   No wonder it's hard for her, bechari.

Faiza   I know. it'll mean we won't get to see each other much. Not that it matters any more.

Faiza *losing appetite.*

Zoya   Kyu?

Faiza   She doesn't want to talk to me again.

Zoya   Nahi, this can't be.

Faiza   It's what she said, her last words to me. And she's stuck to every word.

Zoya   How long has it been?

Faiza   Months –

Zoya   Bring her in here next time, let me talk to her –

Iqra *giggles.*

Zoya   Kyu has-re-ho?

Iqra   How will she bring her here if she's not talking to her huh?

Zoya   Where does she live?

Iqra   Stop trying to fix everyone's problems, Zoya!

Faiza   We'd spend Christmas and New Year's together every year. This year will be the first time we don't . . .

Iqra   And whose fault is that eh? Trotting off to Alaska!

Faiza   But I wanted to be with her, spend every moment, but she won't let me in. She threw out my clothes, my things, the toys I had as a kid. Things we got from here. (*Takes the shop in.*)

Zoya   What about your papa? Can't he do something, say something to her –

Faiza   He's tried, but he's caught between us – it's not fair on him. It makes him ill, I can see it, so I've just left it . . . it's the best thing for everyone. I think something happened to make her the way she is.

Zoya   What was it?

Faiza   I don't know.

Iqra   How can you speculate like that? Without talking to her.

Faiza   I've tried.

Zoya   Have you?

Faiza (*uneasy*)   Of course.

Zoya   It'll be harder than you realise – leaving her.

Faiza   But it feels like I already have, or she's left me.

Zoya   I would do anything to have my ammi here. if she was here, I'd eat with her, every iftari, every sehri. I'd feed her –

Faiza   I would if I could, she doesn't want that –

Zoya   How do you know? You make her sound like some . . . awful person –

Faiza   She isn't –

Zoya   Of course she isn't. She's your ammi! –

Faiza   And I love her more than anything in this world. That's why it hurts.

A beat. **Zoya** *takes this in.*

Zoya   Allah khair karrai. I'll do dua for you and her inshallah. It will improve, with time.

Iqra   / Inshallah.

Faiza   Inshallah. Thank you.

A beat.

Faiza   Zoya?

Zoya   Hahn?

Faiza (*a beat*)   This is delicious. (*Pointing to the gobi in her Tupperware.*)

Zoya (*hitting* **Iqra**, *but talking to* **Faiza**)   You're too kind, but it's not as delicious as your mother's, nothing will compare to that.

Faiza (*turns to* **Zoya**)   What did your mum make for you?

Zoya   Ammi? She made everything. Biryani, keema, gosht ki chawal, pillau, zarda, motth-ki daal, no one made daal like her, we'd bite our fingers off. (*Snapping out of it.*) We should get back –

Iqra   Nahi, the food's barely touched my sides.

Faiza   We have time, don't we?

Zoya   Breaks are short, Woolies will only get busier –

Faiza   You must miss her, your ammi.

Zoya   She's there, I'm here, I'll see her again one day –

Faiza   It's funny how you can be so far away from your mum but feel so close, and I can feel so far away from mine even though she's right here.

Zoya   I never think about how far away it is.

Faiza   It's like you had no choice but to come here and leave her –

Iqra *can see* **Zoya** *feeling unnerved.*

Iqra   Acha theek hai. Let's go back to work.

Zoya   She wanted me to come here, she could see it was the best thing –

Faiza   Is it?

Zoya   What?

Faiza   The best thing for who?

Zoya   What's it to you?

Iqra   Zoya. Aram karo ji.

A beat. **Zoya** *abruptly rises.*

Zoya   I'm getting back to work.

Faiza *rises and tries to get* **Zoya***'s attention.*

Faiza   I'm sorry if I upset you. I didn't mean to.

Zoya *stonewalls* **Faiza***.*

Iqra (*to* **Faiza**)   Don't worry. I know what to do.

Zoya *refills the pick n mix.* **Iqra** *stands beside.*

Iqra   Eat some Zoya, now your roza's open, sweeten your tongue.

Iqra *reaches for a sweet.* **Zoya** *holds her hand, pinches her skin.*

Iqra   *Aiii.* (*Releasing her finger.*) Kutti!

Zoya   How many times –

Iqra   They won't notice one or two missing –

Zoya   It will drop! Of course, they will.

Iqra   Then refill, yaar, it's your job.

Zoya   It's the principle! Don't you get it. It's theft –

Iqra   What about the kameena kiddies with their snotty fingers. Everyone does it, yaar –

Zoya   What will be left? Don't be selfish, Iqra.

Iqra   I've fasted the entire day and I need a bit of meetha to sweeten my tongue, and you do too.

Zoya   I need to work, you do too.

Iqra (*sings*)   'A spoonful of sugar helps the medicine go down'

Zoya *releases a smile.* **Iqra** *spots it.*

Iqra   I know you, Zoya, *tum ko ghar yaad aaraha hay.*

Zoya   I need to work.

Iqra   *Acha theek hai*, let me buy a bag.

Zoya   Stop being silly, I have no time for this.

Iqra   If you won't eat it, I will. Faiza hasn't even had her first pick n mix bechari, ajao kurree –

Faiza   I've never had pick n mix.

Iqra *gasps excessively.*

Zoya   Yeh kya drameh –

Faiza   I wasn't allowed – it wasn't worth the price –

Iqra (*to* **Zoya**)   Pass us a bag then, come on, jaldi kar!

Zoya   You can take it yourself.

Iqra (*gasps*)   What was it you said? Customers are always right? Kya hua?

Zoya *passes* **Iqra** *the bag.* **Iqra** *doesn't take it.* **Iqra** *stares at* **Faiza**.

Iqra   *Is ko doh.*

A beat. **Zoya** *gives the bag to* **Faiza**. **Faiza** *takes it.*

Iqra   Which sweets shall we have? Which ones do you want, Faiza?

Faiza *stares at them all, overwhelmed, triggered. A beat.* **Iqra** *and* **Zoya** *watch her.*

Faiza   I think I'm good, honestly, I'm feeling full.

Iqra   No pick! This is on me. (*A beat.*) Go on Zoya, which ones should she have?

Zoya   What's got into you? –

Iqra   Is this how you talk to customers?

Faiza   We should probably get back to work –

Zoya   She's right –

Iqra   Nahi! –

Faiza   I don't feel like any sweets, not right now.

Iqra   Kya hua?

Zoya   You might like the butterscotch fudge.

Faiza   What?

Zoya   It's nice and soft and crumbly . . . I've heard.

Iqra   Achaa, pass it here then. Come on. Chop chop!

Zoya *passes the picker to* **Iqra**. **Iqra** *passes it to* **Faiza**. **Faiza** *pours it in.*

Zoya   Once you've had that maybe you could have something like the liquorice –

Iqra   Oh chorro. No one likes that one –

Faiza   I don't mind it, I actually quite like it –

Zoya (*smiles, opens lid*)   Then put some in.

Then some chocolate, I like this one, it's richer, but most people like that one because it's sweeter.

Faiza   I'll have that one.

Zoya *smiles.* **Zoya** *is in her element now.*

Zoya   I would still have the sweeter one but that's after the mint – it freshens the mouth – when you bite into it, it's creamy.

Iqra *smiles and steps away from them discreetly.*

Zoya   And of course, you can't forget the white chocolate mice. But you mustn't have it after the mint, you'll have to change the order.

Faiza   Do I always eat it in this order?

Zoya   Yes of course! Aur kya?

Faiza (*amused*)   Did you come up with this?

Zoya   Me and Iqra – (*Turns around.*)

Faiza   When did you do that?

Zoya   Where is she? And the cola fizzy bottles. Those are her favourites.

Faiza *puts some in.*

Faiza   Is everything okay with Iqra?

Zoya   Hahn. Kyu?

Faiza   I don't know. It's just –

Zoya   What did I say. Like rusk to chai. Put more in, she won't leave you any. Do you like toffee?

Faiza   Yes of course, do you?

Zoya *nods cheekily. She points to it to suggest she puts it in.*

Zoya   Not too much of these / they're bad for your teeth.

Faiza   They're bad for your teeth.

Zoya *and* **Faiza** *stare at each other, laugh at this. Then a sudden unexpected blast of music. It's a Bollywood song.*

Zoya   Kutti!

Iqra *suddenly appears out of nowhere like a Bollywood heroine. The song is 'Pardesi Pardesi'.* **Iqra** *lip syncs along to it.*

Zoya   Hai meri Allah. (*Moves towards the storeroom.*)

Iqra *gets in her way, while dancing –*

Iqra   Come on, show us how to dance.

Zoya   Don't tease me, Iqra.

Iqra   Block the door, Faiza. Chalo! Jaldi.

A beat. **Faiza** *stares at them both.*

Iqra   This is what she needs.

Zoya   Tu chup! Iska matlab kya?

Faiza *blocks the door.*

Iqra *sings lyrics from 'Pardesi Pardesi'.*

Zoya   You'll get us all fired with your singing and dancing, hai meri allah! Yeh kya hai?

Iqra   Humai sakaona? Zoya is a first class dancer!

Faiza   Really? I can't tell if you're joking –

Iqra   Show us how you danced at your brother's shaadi.

Zoya   Now's not the time . . . or place –

Iqra   Of course it is –

Zoya   There's customers here!

Iqra   Faiza, dance with me!

Iqra *grabs* **Faiza***'s hand, and dances with her.*

Faiza   I can't dance –

Iqra   You will!

Faiza   Honestly I can't.

Faiza *reluctantly dances with her.* **Zoya** *can't bear to watch them both.*

Zoya   Both of you won't get husbands like this.

Iqra *sings along, but all wrong.*

Zoya   Oh my god, Iqra! Bus kar!

Iqra   What?

Zoya   My ears! You're not singing it right.

Iqra   I am!

Zoya *beautifully sings the lyrics from 'Pardesi Pardesi'.*

Faiza *is shocked, taken aback.*

Faiza   Your voice!

Iqra   It shocked me too, the first time I heard it. Isn't it beautiful? –

Zoya   Chupp kar!

Faiza   It is.

Zoya   You're both dancing wrong –

Iqra   There is no right or wrong!

Zoya   There is – it's like this, look –

Iqra   She taught the entire pind to dance for her bhai's shaadi –

Zoya *teaches them some moves.* **Faiza** *is again stunned.*

Zoya   Tu chupp, are you watching?

They try to copy her moves.

Zoya   That's it Faiza – you're getting it!

Faiza   Am I?

Zoya   Yes! You're good.

Zoya (to **Iqra**)   Iqra, copy her!

Iqra   Now even the desi girl is teaching me to dance –

The three begin to dance synchronised. They acknowledge each other, as this almost comical realisation lands. Then the dance turns joyous and fun, and they let go of the 'right' steps. They relish this moment of letting go. It should be a moment of pure and unadulterated joy, and the moment can go on for as long as it needs to. Until the music abruptly stops. They stop dancing. **Zoya** *is like a deer in headlights. They're in trouble.*

Zoya (*to* **Iqra**)   What have you done?

Four

Moments later. Silence. They're packing up.

Iqra   Nothing will happen, Zoya, stop worrying!

Zoya   I'm leaving, I know it. All because of you.

Iqra   Aram karu ji.

Zoya   Did you not hear what he said? It's the end, I can feel it.

Faiza   He sounded . . . disappointed but there won't be any repercussions I don't think.

Zoya   How do you know that? The way he sees us, me, will change forever –

Iqra (*sarcastic*)   Oh really, oh no?!

Zoya   Shut up!

Iqra   Why does that even bother you? What they think of us?

Zoya   You can afford for it to not bother you.

Iqra Come on yaar – even the goray were dancing, it's a nice change from Mariah.

Zoya Why do you always do this?

Iqra Kya?

Zoya You have your degree, papa ka fortune to fall back on, your friends. What do I have? But this.

A beat.

Iqra I care about this too, Zoya.

Zoya Pfft!

Iqra Of course I do.

Zoya Then why don't you ever show it? You treat it like some playground where you can play your silly games. When will you grow up?

Iqra You had to grow up – that doesn't mean you have to take us there with you!

Zoya You're right.

Iqra Zoya.

Zoya Some people are born with everything, and some people are born with nothing, and if you have everything, how will you ever know what it's like to have nothing, what it's like to have to fight to survive – who can blame you Iqra, for being so . . . naive –

Iqra I work hard Zoya. I won't let you say that I don't. I wake up 5am every day – you know this – I study, read books, write essays and then I do my shifts here – and if it looks like I don't care it's because I'm tired Zoya, there's so much I want to do to change this fucking world, but it's like . . . I can't, no one's listening, no one cares –

Zoya Of course they care. You're at Oxford.

Iqra   If I don't know what it's like to be you, well then you don't what it's like to be me.

Faiza   What is it like? (*A beat.*) Are you okay?

Zoya   Pfft. Don't fall for it Faiza. She wants us to feel sorry for her . . . You do all this; you get us fired / and now you want me to feel sorry for you.

Iqra   You're not getting fired, it's all in your head.

Faiza   I think she was doing this for you.

Iqra   Nahi chorro, Faiza, some people don't know how to be grateful.

Zoya   Doing *what* for me?

A beat.

Faiza   She could see you needed it.

Zoya   Thank you for reminding me, you said that: 'she needs this', please tell me: what do I need? What are you blessing me with, Iqra?

A beat. **Iqra** *doesn't respond.*

Faiza   She could tell you were sad, upset.

Zoya   Why do you keep speaking for her? –

Iqra   You miss home Zoya . . .

Zoya   And you don't? Nahi, you're made of iron, metal. Nothing cuts through Iqra Razwan.

Iqra   Of course I do. All the time.

Zoya   You didn't even say goodbye to them. Your ammi, abbu. Who even does that?

Zoya *turns away from them.*

Faiza   Dancing now, doing what you did at your brother's wedding must've brought back something? Some little bits of joy? You were enjoying yourself –

Iqra   You were, Zoya.

Faiza   I could see it on your face, it meant something to you . . . you were happy –

Iqra   She's right –

Faiza   Maybe it was reliving those good memories? –

Zoya   Memories of what?

Iqra   Your bhai ki shaadi, aur kya?

Zoya   I didn't go . . . I didn't go to his wedding.

Iqra   You said that you did?

Zoya   How could I go? We have no money. We can't afford to fly back. Life moves on without you. People get married, babies are born, people die, life moves.

Iqra   Why did you lie to me?

Zoya   When there's no memories to make, to hold – I thought stories could do that –

Iqra   Oh Zoya –

Zoya   I wanted to believe I was there.

Faiza   This is why you're working here? To pay for you to go back?

Iqra   And you will go back soon . . . create new memories – every year, every summer – I'm sorry.

Zoya   Koi baht nai, I know you were trying to help.

Zoya *reaches for* **Iqra**'s *hand.*

Iqra   I could've helped then, / I can help.

Zoya   This was before I had met you, nahi Iqra, I'll get there.

Iqra   Sachhee? Achaa? August '97.

Zoya   If I went maybe we wouldn't have met.

Faiza   How did you meet?

Iqra   Tell her the story.

Zoya   It was one of the most tragic moments of all of history –

Faiza   What happened?

Zoya   Princess Diana died, Allah rest her soul.

Faiza   Is that it?

Zoya *and* **Iqra** *stare at her in disbelief, sadness.*

Zoya   How do you not feel . . . anything? You were born here. She was your princess.

Faiza   She's not *my* princess.

Iqra *comforting* **Zoya***, they're both too moved to talk.* **Faiza** *is a bit bemused by this –*

Faiza   Are you okay? What's happening here?

Zoya (*to* **Iqra**)   I don't think I can do it –

Iqra   You can.

A beat.

Zoya   Sometimes out of the saddest tragedies beautiful things bloom, like those flowers we left outside Buckingham Palace, they were bilkul the same –

Iqra   These bright pink tulips –

Zoya   Surrounded by a sea of white lilies –

Iqra   Why does everyone get lilies when people die, for her . . . of all people – ugh–

Zoya   But we had the same idea, we came all the way from Oxford, all the way to London, all the way from Pakistan, with the same flowers.

Iqra   She brought us together –

Zoya   I could finally relax after all those months of trying to speak . . . Right then, I could just listen to my own tongue as it flowed with yours. It was like I was back there, in the pind, talking to my sister. D'you remember how I didn't want to leave your side?

Iqra   And you didn't, not really.

Zoya   But you did. You left without saying goodbye.

Iqra   What are you talking about?

Zoya   How do you not remember. She does this. You'll see. Like a ghost. She's here one moment. Gone the next. I see her on the train back. And that's when I took her number. I had nothing to write it on. I memorised it – 01865 491 / 831 (*in-joke jingle*).

Iqra   831. they were good times.

Zoya   When you meet people like that, it's like the whole universe . . . kya nam hai?

Iqra   Aligned –

Zoya   Hanji, 'aligned' itself for you to meet –

Iqra   Alhamdulillah.

Iqra *feels uneasy.* **Faiza** *notices.*

Zoya   Maybe the same is true with you, Faiza.

Faiza   I don't know.

Iqra   Jhoot nahi bol.

Zoya   Out of all the places you could've worked, you ended up here, with us.

Iqra   Why are you so superstitious, Zoya?

Zoya   She didn't trust you –

Iqra   I still don't.

Faiza   It might be mutual.

Iqra (*to* **Zoya**)   When did *you* start trusting her?

Zoya   Chup'nee. You're one of us now, I've decided.

Faiza   / You don't need to say that.

Iqra   Really? Without consulting me.

Zoya   Hahnji –

Iqra   She's only been here five minutes!

Faiza   You barely know me.

Zoya   I don't need to. I . . . just feel something about you, I don't know what it is.

A beat.

Faiza   You do?

Iqra   Because she's a British-born Pakistani –

Zoya   Don't listen to her bakwaas, Faiza . . . You are a kind and caring soul.

Faiza   Thank you!

Zoya   And you should come with us to the Millennium Dome. We're going in the new year. Come with us. That's okay, isn't it? (*Turning to* **Iqra**.)

Iqra   Kyu nahi. (*uneasy*) Ao na. The more the merrier.

Faiza   I'd love to, but I don't think I can.

Zoya   Kyu?

Faiza   In the new year I mean, I won't be around, I'm sorry –

Iqra   She's leaving, remember! To become an artist!

Zoya   Won't you stay a little longer? We're going Blenheim Palace too – ao na. Iqra is showing me all the colleges.

Iqra   Not all, whichever we can get into, we'll see Inshallah –

Zoya Then we'll go Port Meadow, Christ Church Meadows, Shotover.

Iqra She has a list.

Zoya (*takes out list from her purse*)   If you don't write things down, they'll never happen – oh yes and punting, hum punting *ge*, Oxford loge ki tarah –

Iqra *takes the list. Feeling uneasy.*

Zoya There's so much of this little city we haven't seen, but next year, in 2000 we will, zaroor –

Iqra Inshallah –

Zoya Why do you keep saying that? –

Iqra Kya –

Zoya Inshallah? –

Iqra I'm simply seeking Allah's approval of our plans –

Zoya Achaa? –

Faiza *absorbs all of this.*

Zoya (*turns to* **Faiza**)   You're from here, you will show us around before you go– tum town, aur tum gown (*points to* **Iqra**) –

Faiza (*to* **Zoya**)   Your town too.

Zoya Not like you. Not yet. I've only just got here.

Iqra What will she show us? The other side of Cowley Centre?

Faiza I don't think I know this place all that well.

Iqra / see –

Faiza And like I said, I won't be (*here*) –

Zoya How can you not know this place?

Faiza It never really felt like my city.

Zoya   But you were born here!

Faiza   I know but . . . it's just –

Zoya   If you never felt like it was yours, then how can it ever be ours? (*Shivering.*)

Faiza*'s attention shifts to the snow globe, she holds it. It glows.*

We gradually drift from the inside of the shop to the outside. They're in winter coats. It's freezing cold.

Iqra   Tum ko thand lagrahi hai, Zoya? Your body still hasn't acclimatised?

A beat.

Zoya   Kya matlab?

Iqra   Acclimatised. *A c c l i m a t i s e d.* It means . . .

Faiza   It's like to get used to something, like to change and adapt to it.

Zoya   Achaa? Has yours? Acclima –

Iqra *shakes her head.*

Iqra   Nahi, it takes years. I don't want it to.

Zoya   You want to feel the cold forever? What's wrong with you? It will snow today.

Iqra   You say that bilkul every day, Zoya.

Zoya   But today it will. (*To* **Faiza**.)   Can you feel it? Do you feel it in your jism?

Faiza   When does this stop?

A beat. It should begin to feel dreamy.

Iqra   She's lying.

Zoya   She can barely talk, bechari –

Faiza (*teeth chatter*)   It's freezing.

Iqra   But you don't feel it like we do. You were born here, in the cold, like a polar bear in ice –

Zoya   If she feels cold let her say she's cold, what's it to you?

Iqra   You better get used to it, if you're going to Alaska, painting the skies –

Faiza   It's colder here than –

Iqra   Than there?

Faiza   No. Than the future.

Zoya   Achaa? The future gets warmer?

A beat.

Faiza   Bit by bit, year by year.

Iqra   There's something to look forward to?

Faiza   The world is slowly burning, that's our fault. We're slowly burning inside it –

Zoya   Who?

Faiza   Me and you.

Zoya and **Faiza** *stare at each other intensely. We should realise we're in* **Faiza**'s *head now –*

Zoya *sings from 'Pardesi Pardesi'.*

Iqra   Aur meh? What about me? What happens to me?

Zoya *continues singing.*

Faiza   I'm trying to savour all this like those toffees we like, but I don't think I can –

Zoya   Kyu?

Faiza   Knowing this is all going to end.

Zoya   Everything will end, Faiza.

Faiza   I know but I wish . . . I wish I could just freeze it and hold it.

Zoya   Like a snow globe? –

Faiza   Yes like a snow globe –

Zoya   Ugh, that's boring. Why would you do that for? Haven't you got better things to do, places to be – of all the places you could be, you choose here –

Faiza   I didn't choose to be here. It chose me. And I'm happy that it did. Cos it's different here, you're different . . . and I like it.

Zoya   Different? Different to what?

Iqra   Different to what you'll become, can't you see.

Zoya   Am I nicer now? Do I turn into some horrible bitch? Huh?

Iqra   You already are one Zoya ji.

Zoya   No I'm not!

Faiza   / You're not –

A beat.

Faiza   It's just you're . . . so happy here, mum! –

A beat. **Zoya** *doesn't know how to respond.*

Faiza   And maybe I don't actually know you. Not properly. It's like you're a different person. And I just don't get it – I don't get what went wrong . . .

A beat. **Faiza** *waits for* **Zoya** *to respond.* **Zoya** *laughs –*

Zoya   How do you still not know?

A beat.

Faiza   What is it? It's like everything's about to change.

Zoya   That's because it is, Faiza –

Faiza   What? What happens? I need to know. Please. Mum?

Zoya   You just like me here because I'm beautiful here, but beauty fades, my girl. Yours will too. (*Smirks.*)

Faiza   Why would you say that?

It's something she would say.

Zoya   There you go! Maybe I was always like that, maybe it was in me all along, this capacity to be unkind, cruel.

Faiza   You were never that, not on purpose I mean, you were just . . .

Zoya   Sad, hanji – you've said that already – a sad little girl! –

Faiza   But here you dance with so much joy and sing, you got this beautiful voice – it's like you have so much talent inside you and you don't ever want to share it, not even with us, and you laugh, and you smile with your teeth and your eyes, and you love this place, and you love your job, and you love . . . Iqra, it's like you have so much of it to give, maybe . . . maybe you used it all up before I came –

Faiza *is waiting for* **Zoya***'s response, but she says nothing. It's like they're both oblivious to her, wrapped up in their own little world.*

Faiza   Zoya? Iqra? . . . Mum?

Faiza *tries to shake the snow globe, but there's no snow inside.* **Faiza** *is bemused, confused.*

Zoya   Ai Faiza –

Faiza *looks up.* **Iqra** *and* **Zoya** *are staring back at her, worried.*

Iqra   There she is –

Faiza   Huh?

Zoya   Where did you go? We thought we lost you there. (*Smiles affectionately.*)

Faiza   Sorry, it's the cold. I think it's done something to me.

Iqra (*rolls her eyes*)   You should be used to it by now.

Faiza   Like a polar bear in ice . . .

Iqra (*confused*)   Kya?

Faiza   Nothing.

Zoya   Come here, take this –

Zoya *passes her a scarf.*

Faiza   I'm fine.

Zoya   You're freezing.

Zoya *wraps the scarf around her.*

Faiza   Thank you.

Zoya   Koi baht nahi. Oh my god, what did I say.

Iqra   Zoya ji can tell the future.

Zoya   Yesterday the skies were pink, it told us everything we needed to know.

They stare at the sky as the snow falls.

Zoya   Isn't it khoobsurat?

Faiza   It really is.

Zoya   I couldn't believe my eyes the first time I saw it fall –

Iqra   We should make a snowman!

Zoya   And freeze our hands, that's a smart idea –

Iqra   Kyu nahi? I want to build a snowman! –

Zoya   There's not even enough snow to make the eyeball of a snowman.

Iqra   But there will be . . . in time.

Zoya   And what about the carrot, and the button and the hat and –

Faiza (*unfurls scarf*)   We could use this.

Zoya   Nahi keep that on, you're cold.

Iqra   We'll use your dupatta, wrap her inside it.

Zoya   Her?

Faiza   A snow woman? –

Zoya   It can't be.

Faiza   Why not?

Iqra   Bilkul a snow-woman from Pakistan – full of songs and hopes and dreams . . .

Zoya   That'll melt eventually.

Iqra   Nahi –

Zoya   Everything melts in the end.

Iqra   We'll keep her frozen.

Zoya   How will you do that?

Faiza   If we keep adding more snow!

A beat.

Zoya   Achaa, girls, meh jahrahai ho.

Iqra   Where are you going?

Zoya   Home! Aur kya?

Faiza   Already?

Iqra   What about our snowman?

Faiza   Won't you stay a little longer?

Zoya   I need to start cooking sehri for Jamal, kal ki iftaari –

Iqra   What are we having tomorrow? Make zarda!

Zoya   Let me see what I can do.

Zoya *hugs* **Faiza**, *then* **Iqra**.

Zoya   Remember your pick n mix!

Faiza *opens the pick n mix bag.*

Faiza   Have some.

Zoya   Nahi, it's yours.

Iqra   Remember to put one pound twenty in the till kal, achaa.

Iqra (*picks it up*)   99p –

Zoya (*picks it up to weigh*)   One pound twenty –

Iqra *takes out the cola bottles and puts it in her mouth.*

Iqra   99p hogai.

Zoya *tuts, as she takes out a toffee and eats it.* **Faiza** *takes one too, savours it.*

Iqra   Don't let the carol singers kidnap you.

Zoya *sings lyrics from 'Last Chrstmas'.*

Iqra   / Beghirat, singing with a full mouth! It's not even a carol –

Zoya *continues singing.*

Zoya   Khudafis.

Faiza   Khudafis!

Zoya *leaves them. They watch her go. The rest of 'Last Christmas' trails off until they can't hear her again.* **Faiza** *stares at* **Iqra**, *almost giving her a death stare. A beat.*

Faiza   When are you going to tell her?

Iqra   What are you talking about?

Faiza   That you're leaving her?

A beat. **Iqra** *is taken aback.*

Faiza   The longer you leave it, the harder it'll be. For the both of you.

Iqra   *Bakwaas band kar.* I knew there was something wrong with you.

Faiza   I know now what breaks her . . . it's you, Iqra. You break her.

Iqra   Chup! Nothing could break her – you don't know her. Stop talking about her like you know her.

Faiza   You only know this part of her – I know the part that comes after –

Iqra   What's wrong with you? –

Faiza   She adores you –

Iqra   Chupp kar –

Faiza   You'll never do any of those things on that list with her, and you know that.

Iqra   You don't know that –

Faiza   Then tell me I'm wrong –

Iqra   You know nothing –

Faiza   You leave her life, you never look back . . . it's about to happen, how did I not realise it til now. That's why I'm here. To witness what's about to happen.

Iqra   I don't know who you are, or what you want from us, but you need to leave us the fuck alone –

Faiza   '*Us*'? (*Laughs.*)

I'll tell you who I am.

I'm the future, I'm Zoya's daughter.

A beat. **Iqra** *smirks.*

Iqra   You need psychiatric help.

Faiza   But the thing is I don't know who you are –

Iqra   You stay the fuck away from me.

Faiza   I never actually meet you. You fucked off to go to Sindh Madressatul Islam University in 2000 –

Iqra   You've been looking through my stuff –

Faiza   Next year you'll learn how to become a Pakistani hot shot politician and stand in the next general election, but you'll also reignite a love with an old flame –

Iqra   Shut up!

Faiza   In the only letter you ever send to her you mention him – Yousef – you talk about how one night, on the beach, as the sun dips into the sea, he proposes to you, and you'll say –

Iqra   Bus! –

Faiza   You don't want to know about how the rest of your life will unfold? Nahi? Kyu nahi?

Iqra   Why are you doing this?

Faiza   Fair enough. (*zips her mouth*) I'll leave you with a few surprises. After everything you two do together – you teaching her to read – *Harry Potter and the Philosophers Stone* – her teaching you to sew and knit – that pink scarf with different shades of pink, and this tiny thread of yellow – you just . . . go. She doesn't know her life's about to change forever, because of you.

Iqra   Does she know her daughter turns into a scary mad woman who terrorises people?

Faiza   At least I don't leave her, and . . . never look back. (*uneasy*)

A beat.

Faiza   You never say goodbye. Just like you left your parents. Just like that day in London. Why do you keep leaving without saying goodbye?

Iqra   You don't know what I'll do – you can't punish me for something I haven't done –

Faiza   Yet . . .? what will you do? Go on.

A beat.

Iqra   It's just one year. A year in Karachi. That's it.

Faiza   Then what?

Iqra   Then . . . I'll be back –

Faiza   One year turns into two, two turns into three, three turns into –

Iqra   I wouldn't do that.

Faiza   You leave her, you leave her fucking unmoored –

Iqra   I would never do that.

Faiza   You already have. I don't know you, I only know the stories she tells.

Iqra   She said she'd go back to Pakistan, every summer. That's what this job is for.

Faiza   That never happens.

Iqra   She stays here, I stay there?

Faiza *nods.* **Iqra** *takes that in.*

Iqra   It doesn't need to be that way.

Faiza   Will you stay here?

Iqra   Will *you* stay here?

Faiza   What?

Iqra   Will you stay here your whole life – and never leave – for her?

Iqra *awaits* **Faiza**.

Iqra   Bol-na, answer me!

A beat. **Faiza** *evades her.*

Iqra   Don't ask me questions you can't answer yourself.

Faiza   It's your fault she turned into this. You did this to her – your inability to face responsibility, your inability to take a moment to say goodbye, to explain.

Iqra   You know the future, do you? Let me ask you something:

Do they ever begin to like us?

Faiza   Who?

Iqra   Them. Cos they don't like us now. There's no place for me here. There isn't.

Faiza   You need to tell her, Iqra.

A beat. **Iqra** *takes this in.*

Iqra   What do I tell her?

A beat.

Faiza   . . . that you're leaving her.

Her own words echo back to her. A sound from the heavens snaps **Faiza**'s *attention. She looks up, terrified, it's too soon to go back. Is this what she felt before she got here?*

Darkness. End Of Act One.

Act Two

Five

An old Punjabi folk song plays – 'Mawan te Dhiyan Ral'. We see a snow woman wrapped in a dupatta slowly melting, as the trio surround her, and add handfuls of snow to her to keep her frozen and intact. Pick n mix sweets are used as the eyes, nose, mouth etc. They wrap **Iqra**'s *pink scarf around it. There's an obvious tension between* **Iqra** *and* **Faiza** *which* **Zoya** *is oblivious to.* **Zoya** *leaves.*

Iqra *and* **Faiza** *step into Woolworths. They're working on Christmas Eve. The rush of Christmas is here.*

Faiza Do we have any more Sweet Treats Barbies? there's a lady who needs it for her daughter. It's her Christmas present –

Iqra Have you checked the back?

Faiza Yes –

Iqra And? –

Faiza *shakes her head.*

Iqra Khatam hogai? –

Faiza What do I tell her? –

Iqra What you just told me . . . the truth.

Faiza She's desperate for it.

Iqra That's not our problem, she should've come sooner, it's Christmas Eve –

Faiza It's what her daughter wanted. She was excited for it all year!

Iqra We don't always get what we want. She'll survive –

Faiza You make it sound so flippant –

Iqra   That's because it's a toy, a gift can be replaced –

Faiza   It can't just be replaced. It'll stay with them, leave a mark –

Iqra (*sarcastic*)   Oh no! Spoiling your child does more harm than good.

Faiza   Are you talking from experience?

Iqra   It's an important lesson to learn early – you won't always get what you want.

A beat.

Faiza   Where is she?

Iqra   You're the future, tum batao.

Faiza   She wouldn't miss Christmas Eve –

Iqra *knows this is true. A beat.*

Faiza   Did you tell her?

Iqra   Kya?

Faiza   Who I am.

Iqra   What impression did I give you that I'm entertaining your mental illness –

Faiza   Because we can't tell her – it could change everything.

Iqra   Isn't that what you want?

Faiza   One misstep could change all our futures. You just need to tell her the truth.

Iqra   Are you gonna break the news to Barbie mummy, or you leaving her waiting? She won't find it anywhere at this rate.

A beat. **Faiza** *goes.*

Iqra *watches her go. She is genuinely worried for* **Zoya**. **Iqra** *picks up the snow globe – and shakes it. It still doesn't hold snow. She is perturbed. She glances at it closely. The pick n mix sweet boxes are running low, she refills them, but they scatter and disperse.* **Faiza** *returns. They both continue to work in silence.*

Faiza   She got something else in the end, instead of the Barbie.

Iqra   Kya ta?

Faiza *shows her. It's a gooey alien egg. She lets it wobble in her fingers.* **Iqra** *is freaked out.*

Iqra   Keep that disgusting thing away from me –

Faiza   The alien gives birth to a smaller alien.

Iqra (*sarcastic*)   Of course it does –

Faiza   And when the new millennium comes, the new baby alien will come to full life.

Iqra   Kya bakwaas, and she still bought it? –

Faiza (*nods*)   She got two –

Iqra   You're just like her, selling ice to Eskimos –

Faiza   Woolies had *everything* you could ever want, all in one place. It's incredible.

Iqra   You make it sound like it's not there anymore.

A beat.

Faiza   What?

Iqra   'It *had* everything' –

Faiza   My bad, it *has* everything I mean –

Iqra (*confused*)   My bad? Michael Jackson ki 'bad'?

Faiza   I mean 'my mistake' . . .

Iqra Is this what language reduces itself to: 'my bad'. how did you get here?

Faiza   What do you mean?

Iqra Woolies? 1999? Right here –

Faiza I don't know –

Iqra *Pfft*! Achaa –

Faiza But I don't. Not really. I kept having the same dream every night.

Iqra Of what?

Faiza The end. The end of 1999. New Year's Eve . . . Me, you . . . her. Standing outside in the cold. Watching the fireworks, shooting into the sky. All these bright colours bursting through the dark, and then I just . . . go.

Iqra Where? Where do you go?

Faiza I don't know. All I saw was you two. It's like I vanished.

Iqra What are you? An apparition? –

Faiza I kept seeing the same thing night after night until –

Iqra How do you know you actually go back?

Faiza What?

Iqra What if you stay? Stay stuck here forever?

Faiza But I won't, I can't stay here . . .

Iqra What happens to us? You never answered me. I want an answer.

Faiza What do you mean?

Iqra Y'know, as an ummah. Muslims. Do they ever begin to . . . like us?

A beat. **Faiza** *doesn't know how to respond.* **Iqra** *can see her reaction – that it's not positive.*

Iqra   Why so serious? Kya matlab? People don't even find us . . . hot in the future? We don't even become desirable to them?

Faiza   Does that matter? –

Iqra   I'm just asking –

Faiza *(sarcastic)*   Oh no, people love us. They really do where I'm from –

Iqra   They do? Mashallah!

Faiza   Can't you feel how loved I am? Life just gets better and better.

Iqra   Then I have something to look forward to? I needn't get into power to change things. Everything will be just . . .fine? *(Sighs, dejected.)*

Faiza   Even though I hate that you left her like that.

Iqra   I haven't done it yet! –

Faiza   It's good what you're doing, Iqra –

Iqra   Don't! –

Faiza   What?

Iqra   I don't want to know what happens.

A beat.

Faiza *(nods)*   What would you do? In power? As PM?

Iqra   Well, okay. Where do I start. I would make sure Kashmir became its own independent state, not a part of us, or India – it needs autonomy, self-governance. And once the world could see what that looked like, then the same could be replicated elsewhere . . . Like Palestine. It's disappearing bit by bit. Palestinian land, their homes. The people. It's heartbreaking.

A beat. **Faiza** *is heartbroken at the thought.* **Iqra** *notices.*

Iqra   What is is it? It doesn't get worse than this?

Faiza *finds it too hard to speak. A beat.* **Zoya** *walks in, she seems a bit stunned.*

Iqra   *Wo aa guy.*

Where were you? we were worried sick –

Faiza (*to* **Iqra**)   Were you? (*To* **Zoya**.) Are you okay?

Iqra   Kee hoya ji?

Zoya   Kuch be nahi. Yeh dekho. (*Acknowledging pick n mix.*) Did a bomb go off in here?

Iqra   What's wrong with it?

Zoya   Christmas Eve of all days, hai meri Allah.

Iqra   That's your fault for abandoning us like that without so much as a warning –

Faiza *smirks at the irony of this.* **Zoya** *tries to clean the mess, and refill them neatly.*

Faiza   It hasn't been the same without you.

Zoya   Hanji, clearly, I can see that.

Iqra   We managed just fine. It's only been a few days.

Zoya   I thought you were 'worried' about me?

Iqra   Of course I am. Look at you. You look terrible.

Faiza   Don't listen to her, you look fine, are you okay?

Zoya   Yes! Thank you for asking, Faiza –

Iqra   Why won't you just tell us. This isn't like you . . . keeping things–

Faiza (*quietly*)   Look who's talking.

Iqra   Chupp karr –

Zoya (*to* **Iqra**)   Kya matlab? (*To* **Faiza**.) What do you mean?

A beat. **Faiza** *and* **Iqra** *glance at one another.*

Faiza   Nothing –

Zoya *feels nauseous – suddenly the sweets scatter.*

Iqra   Oh hor, now look who's making mess.

Faiza   You should sit down.

Faiza *rushes towards* **Zoya**, *holds her by the hand.* **Zoya** *smiles, appreciates the gesture.*

Zoya   Thank you.

Iqra   Roza hai, aaj?

Zoya *shakes her head.*

Iqra   Kya hua?

Faiza   Here. Maybe we should stop interrogating her.

She draws up a chair for her.

Zoya   Thank you.

Faiza   Can I get you something?

Iqra   Bol na, Zoya!

Zoya   I'm pregnant.

Iqra   Oh Zoya.

Iqra *glances at* **Faiza** *then* **Iqra**, *she's doing the maths.* **Iqra** *laughs in amazement.* **Faiza** *averts her gaze.*

Iqra   Oh my god!

Zoya   Kyu has-re ho?

Iqra *notices* **Zoya**'*s muted expression.*

Iqra   Tum theek ho na Zoya?

Zoya *nods.* **Iqra** *stands next to her and holds her head against her.*
Zoya *allows herself to be embraced.* **Faiza** *observes all this, taking
it in.*

Iqra   Everything will be fine, okay, inshallah.

Zoya   Inshallah?

Iqra   You've been sick?

Zoya *nods.* **Iqra** *strokes her hair.*

Iqra   Bechari.

Faiza   Can I get you some water or something?

Zoya *shakes her head.* **Iqra** *voices no to* **Faiza***.*

Faiza   I'm sure it will pass in time.

Iqra   It will, zaroor.

Zoya   I don't know.

Iqra   You poor baby.

Zoya   I'll be okay.

Iqra   Does Jamal know?

Zoya   Abi nahi.

Iqra   Your family?

Zoya *shakes her head.*

Iqra   Why didn't you come to me?

Zoya   I didn't know what to do.

Faiza   What do you mean?

Zoya   I knew this would happen. I wanted it to happen . . .
but.

A beat. **Faiza** *is shocked.* **Iqra** *glances at her.*

Iqra   It's a lot to take in. Give yourself time.

Zoya   You get married, you have bachai, you build a family, grow the khandan. This is what was meant to happen.

Faiza   Is it what you want?

A beat. **Zoya** *doesn't know how to answer.* **Faiza** *processes it all.*

Zoya   I don't know.

Iqra   You're overwhelmed. Go home, get some rest. We'll manage here.

Zoya   Nahi. Tomorrow's Christmas. They need me here –

Iqra   They'll understand, you won't lose your job –

Zoya   You don't know that.

Iqra   Woolies can wait. You need to look after yourself Zoya.

Zoya   Stop fussing over me. Both of you.

Iqra (*to* **Faiza**)   Maybe *this* is what broke her.

Faiza   What?

Iqra   Not me, but . . . you. Can't you see –

A beat. **Faiza**, *upset, holds the baby alien tightly, comfortingly, stares at it. And then abruptly leaves.*

Iqra   Faiza.

Zoya   What's wrong with her?

Iqra   Come back.

Zoya   What did you say to her? Is she okay?

Iqra *stops* **Faiza** *from going.*

Iqra   We need you here. Don't we, Zoya?

Zoya   Kyu nahi? 'Course we do.

Faiza   You're just saying that.

Zoya   No I'm not. Especially as someone as thoughtful and skilled as you. Today of all days. You're good at this.

Faiza   I don't get it. Is not even a small part of you . . . happy about this?

Zoya   Happy? –

Faiza   Or hopeful? I don't know, it's just . . .

Iqra   She will be in time, I'm sure of it.

Zoya   I don't know how I feel. It's all happening too fast.

Iqra   These things take time to settle.

Zoya   This will change my life –

Faiza   In every terrible way?! –

Iqra   Faiza! –

Zoya   It's not some tiny toy you can drop whenever you're bored –

Faiza   Don't you think I know that? –

Zoya   Kya matlab? –

Faiza   Doesn't matter – .

Zoya   It's one whole human being / with thoughts, feelings –

Faiza   That you don't even want?

Zoya   What if they don't want me?

Faiza   What? –

Zoya   They might not want me, and can I blame them? Who would?

Iqra   Zoya! What did I say!

Zoya   Kya?

Iqra   Stop talking like this about yourself.

Faiza   You'll be . . . their mother, of course they'd *want* you.

Zoya How can you be so sure?

Faiza Every child wants their mother.

Zoya Is that how it works?

Faiza A child loves who brings them into this world –

Zoya So I don't even have to be . . . good to earn their love? How is that fair?

Faiza I don't understand.

Zoya Are you ready? –

Faiza What? –

Zoya To be a mother?

(*To* **Iqra**.) Or you? Bol na –

Iqra Nahi –

Zoya Kya? –

Iqra Nahi! –

Zoya Achaa. But you expect me to . . . Is it because when you look at me, you don't see what else I could be, but this thing that gives life to something else.

Faiza No! You're so much more than that. You'll always be more than that.

Iqra With your dreams and hopes.

Zoya Where do they go now?

Iqra They don't need to change, Zoya.

Zoya You make it sound so easy. But I have to bring them into this world, keep them safe, happy, fed . . . loved – me.

Iqra You'll have me. Have you forgotten that, eh? I will help you every step of the way, I promise. We'll do this together.

Zoya I know but –

Faiza   How can you promise that?

Iqra   Chupp kar –

Faiza   Are you staying now? –

Zoya   What do you mean, 'staying' –

Faiza   Why are you lying for? –

Zoya   Kya?

Iqra   Zoya.

Zoya   Hahn.

Iqra   Faiza has something to tell you –

Faiza   Don't do this –

Zoya   Tell me what?

Iqra   She's panicking!

Zoya   What is it? –

Faiza   It'll make it worse –

Iqra   She needs to know.

Zoya   Know what?

Iqra   Zoya.

Faiza   Stop it –

Iqra   Do you know who this is?

Zoya   What is this? –

Faiza   Please! –

Iqra (*to* **Faiza**)   Tell her, Faiza –

Zoya   Who are you?

A beat.

Iqra   She's growing inside you.

Faiza   Don't listen to her!

Iqra   She's your daughter. She's from the future.

A beat. It should feel achingly long. **Zoya** *is stunned.* **Zoya** *laughs hysterically. The pair watch her.*

Zoya   You two are funny! I never thought I'd see the day you would . . . (*Laughs.*)

Faiza   Zoya –

Zoya   I leave you for two days and you . . .

A beat.

Zoya   I come here and tell you something I haven't told anyone, this thing that will change my life forever, and you scheme and tease me with your . . . stupid jokes.

Iqra   This isn't a stupid joke Zoya.

Faiza   Just drop it now.

Iqra   I didn't believe her either, not at first.

Zoya *trails off.*

Iqra (*to* **Faiza**)   Give her time. It's a lot to take in.

Faiza   You shouldn't have said anything, why did you tell her?

Iqra   She needs to know everything will be fine.

Faiza   You don't know that.

Iqra   You turned out okay.

Faiza   Did I?

Iqra   She needs to know that she'll survive, that she'll be okay in the end –

Faiza   What if . . . she isn't?

Iqra   You know that's not true.

Faiza   Do I? Cos the truth is I don't think she is fine. Not really, and maybe that's *my* fault, you were right. It wasn't you. It was me.

Iqra   I didn't mean that Faiza–

Faiza   It's true –

Iqra   We can change things –

Faiza   How?

Iqra   The future is still ahead of us –

Faiza   For you, not me.

Iqra   Zoya idar ao!

Faiza   What are you doing? –

Iqra   Zoya!

Faiza   Stop this please.

Zoya *comes to them with stock –*

Zoya   What have you schemed together now?

Iqra   I woudn't do this to you after something like this.

Zoya   Nahi?

Iqra   And you know that.

Go on, (*encourages* **Faiza** *to speak*) Bol-na –

Make her believe you are who you say you are.

Zoya   I wouldn't name my daughter 'Faiza', what does that even mean?

Faiza   It means successful, beneficial –

Zoya   Ugh –

Faiza   Abbu named me –

Zoya   Abbu?! Jamal? You're funny. I wouldn't let Jamal name my first child.

Faiza   I thought you didn't want it –

Zoya   Did I say that? (*Turns to* **Iqra**.) Did I say that? Who are you? What do you want from us?

Iqra   Zoya, araam se.

Faiza   I'm only here until the millennium –

Zoya   Where will you go?

Faiza   Back to . . . where I came from.

Zoya   The future? Of course.

Iqra   You're getting it.

Zoya   How did you end up here?

Faiza   I don't know.

Iqra   It's the dreams Zoya.

Zoya   Tu chupp.

Iqra   Mein kee keeta hai?

Faiza   I woke up here. In the same house. But everything's different, changed, it's 1999.

Zoya   Kahaan?

Faiza   Cowley –

Zoya   We stay in Cowley? Achaa.

Iqra   It could be worse, Blackbird Leys, Barton –

Zoya   Jehrico be hai, Headington –

Faiza   You always wanted to move there, especially when we went secondary school 'cos you wanted me to go Cherwell – but those areas are expensive, and abbu liked Cowley. I thought you liked it too –

Zoya   I don't know what makes you think you know me Faiza, or makes you think you can just . . . use me to process your feelings towards her – (*Beat.*) The way you talk about her –

Iqra   Kaun?

Zoya   Her . . . mother. She makes her sound like this horrible / human being.

Faiza   She isn't horrible . . . you're not, mum, / I never meant it like that –

Zoya   Don't call me that –

Faiza   I'm sorry –

Zoya   You were right, Iqra. Paghal hai. She needs help, bechari –

Faiza   There's nothing wrong with me –

Zoya   Stop talking to me –

Faiza   Mum? Please listen to me–

Iqra   Zoya –

Zoya (*to* **Iqra**)   Keep her away from me –

Iqra   Faiza, that's enough, bus –

Faiza   Why won't you just listen to me? –

Zoya   Stop talking to me –

Faiza *sings from the song 'Mawan te Dhiyan Ral'.*

A beat. **Zoya** *is speechless.*

Faiza   They sang it at your rukksati – your ammi, chaachis, khaalas, phuppos, clapping their hands, the dhol as they watched you leave out their door –

A beat.

Zoya   You were there too? My past and my future?

Faiza   No but your sisters were – Rubina jaan and Khadija bibi – they were too little to understand all this, what the song meant. And you didn't want them to know what would one day happen to them. You sneaked out and bought them piste kulfi 'cos you felt guilty you were leaving them. And your mum thought you'd changed your mind, and what you wanted to say to her was: I don't get it – how can I just leave you like this – but instead you just smiled, and said 'thank you ammi' –

Zoya *processes this gradually* –

Faiza   That night you cried yourself to sleep at the thought of how you'd survive here in the cold without her.

A beat. **Zoya** *takes it in slowly.*

Faiza   But you did, you did survive. You raised four children – who adore the bones of you.

A beat. **Zoya** *is taken aback.*

Six

The leitmotif of Pardesi Pardesi appears, until it gets louder and louder.

It's Boxing Day. **Zoya** *stares out at the Santa display, lost in thought.* **Iqra** *joins her side.*

Zoya   I know what's wrong with him –

Iqra   Kaun?

Zoya (*gestures*)   Santa sahb.

Iqra   Kya hai?

Zoya   Iskee smile –

Iqra *watches closely.*

Iqra   It looks fine to me.

Zoya   You said 'what isn't wrong with it'.

Iqra   Yeh mazaak tha.

Zoya   You made me think it was kharaab –

Iqra   How could you not tell that I didn't mean it –

Zoya   But you're wrong, wrong now, right then . . . even if you didn't mean it. The moment we have to take him down, it all begins to make sense –

Iqra   Abi nahi, we can keep it up a little longer –

Zoya   Christmas has come and gone –

Iqra   Kya baat hai? what's wrong with him?

Zoya   He's smiling with his lips, his mouth –

Iqra   Aur kya? Not with his teeth? –

Zoya   Not with his eyes. A real smile holds your eyes. Aankhein.

Iqra *sings a lyric from the song 'Ankhein Milane Wale'. She waits for* **Zoya** *to complete it.*

Iqra *awaits* **Zoya** *to complete it.*

Iqra   Santa's eyes look smiley –

Zoya   Nahi . . . they look sad, scared –

Iqra   What would Santa be scared of? Delivering all those presents for those children in one night.

Zoya (*heavy sigh*)   Bahut bari responsibility hai –

Iqra   Bilkul, and yet he still manages, year after year. Why won't you talk to her?

Zoya   I can't understand anything. Nothing is making sense.

Iqra   You're scared of what she knows, but she doesn't need to tell us everything, she can help us.

Zoya   With what?

Iqra   The future, with what's ahead –

Zoya   We can't just miss all the bad bits, look for the good bits –

Iqra   Kyu nahi?

Zoya   Life isn't like that.

Faiza *arrives with stock.* **Zoya** *avoids* **Faiza***, doesn't talk to her.*

Faiza   I didn't know where to put this.

A beat, **Iqra** *waits for* **Zoya***, and then steps forward instead.*

Iqra (*steps forward*)   That can go on aisle two.

Faiza (*discreetly to* **Iqra**)   It's like she's turning into her, day by day.

Iqra   Kya? –

Faiza   Mum –

Iqra   It's all in your head.

Faiza   If we don't do something now, we'll be stuck like this forever.

Iqra   Chupp kar.

Faiza   Nothing will change. I haven't got time –

Zoya   Give it here.

Zoya *steps towards* **Faiza***, and hands her the box –* **Zoya** *takes her in for the first time. She takes some of the stock out –*

Zoya   It's all reduced, so it should go at the front so everyone can see. Separate them into different sections. Girls. Boys. Men. Women. Mothers.

Faiza   Thank you!

Zoya   Tum bhi karu. (*Calling out to* **Iqra**.)

Iqra (*eyes roll*)   Theek hai.

Zoya   50% off these. 30% off these. These can stay the same price. They'll still be popular with the aunties. They like boxing day cheapies.

Faiza *releases a smile. The three work together in silence, glancing at one another.* **Zoya.**

Begins to take **Faiza** *in more, every part of her.* **Iqra** *watches the pair of them.*

Iqra   There's a resemblance between you –

Zoya   Chupp kar –

Iqra   There is. It's the lips, mouth –

Zoya   Bakwaas band kar –

Iqra   How would you be able to tell Zoya? It takes someone on the outside, to see.

Zoya   Bus kar yaar. People thought we were sisters.

Iqra   Kaun?

Zoya   Hum. Meh aur aap. Don't you remember?

Faiza   I can see that –

Iqra   Who thought that about us?

Zoya   Customers! Aur kaun?

Iqra   We'll look the same to them.

Faiza   The real things that resemble us, no one can see. Like this birthmark that looks like a conker.

Faiza *shows* **Zoya** *that she has it too.* **Zoya** *takes this in, then turns. A beat.*

Zoya   What went wrong?

Iqra   Kya?

Zoya   I'm talking to her.

(*To* **Faiza**.) What went wrong with her . . . Your mum.

Faiza *glances at* **Iqra**, *who evades her glance.* **Zoya** *notices.*

Zoya   Was she always like that? –

Faiza   No, I had a good childhood, a loving one –

Zoya   What happened? –

Iqra   Why do you want to know? What will it do, Zoya? –

Zoya   Tell me –

Faiza   It's like she's . . . triggered.

Zoya   Triggered? (*To* **Iqra**.) Kya matlab? Triggered?

Faiza   It's like sometimes things hits . . . you, her, reminds her about something painful –

Zoya   Like what? What is it?

A beat.

Faiza   Like me going away, moving away.

Zoya   To Alaska?

Faiza   Yeah.

Zoya   Why would that hurt her?

Faiza   I don't know –

Zoya   Yes you do, tell me –

Iqra   Why does it matter, Zoya? –

Zoya   Why would that hurt her? –

Faiza   I think she's used to people leaving her –

Zoya   Who leaves her?

Iqra   Leave it Zoya. You'll drive yourself mad.

Zoya   It's too late for that.

Iqra   Focus on this moment, right now –

Zoya   How often does she go back?

Faiza   Where?

Zoya   Home . . . does she go back? I'm being stupid, ignore me –

Faiza   No, she does, she does go back.

Zoya *sighs with quiet relief, waits on tenterhooks.*

Faiza   . . . a few times.

A beat.

Zoya   A few times? Then she comes back . . . here? She stays here?

Faiza *nods. A beat.* **Zoya** *takes the place in. Woolies. What was it all for.*

Zoya   How many times?

Faiza *counts it on her hand.* **Zoya** *watches.*

Faiza   I think . . . four . . . yes maybe four times.

Zoya *is devastated.*

Zoya   That's it?

Iqra   It's okay, Zoya. Allah khair karrai.

Zoya   How old are you, Faiza? (*Tries to calculate it.*)

Faiza   Twenty-six.

It sinks in for **Zoya**. *She clasps onto* **Iqra** *almost without knowing, for comfort, support.*

Zoya   Four times. In twenty-six years.

Faiza   She found it hard I think, and the later it got, the harder it got, her worries and fears kept changing, she was scared that she became different to them I think.

A beat. **Zoya** *processes this.*

Iqra   Zoya . . .

Zoya   How could that be? All that time. We just stay here? We just stay working here all our lives, til we're old wrinkly bhuddiya! With chitteh safed hair. Aren't you hearing this? Hai, Iqra?

A beat. **Iqra** *doesn't respond.*

Zoya   *Kya hua?*

Iqra   That doesn't happen, Zoya.

Zoya   Kya matlab? If I don't go back, if I don't stay here . . . What happens to us? What happens to this place?

Iqra (*glances at* **Faiza**)   Tell her.

Zoya   Tell me what?

Iqra   Tell her what happens.

A beat.

Faiza   It doesn't exist anymore.

Zoya   Kya?

Faiza   Woolworths – in the future – it doesn't exist.

Zoya *glances at* **Iqra** *in disbelief.*

Iqra   There's something else you need to know –

Iqra *finding it hard.*

Faiza (*to* **Iqra**)   It's okay, you can do this.

Iqra   I'm leaving . . . Zoya, I don't exist in your future.

A long beat. **Zoya** *turns to* **Faiza**.

Faiza   It's true. I don't know her.

Zoya   Why are you making her say these things –

Faiza   I've never met her. Not until I came here.

Zoya *begins to piece this together.*

Zoya   Mein issay nahi jaantee. (*To* **Iqra**.) She's lying, this proves it.

Faiza   You used to talk about her all the time, show me pictures, tell me stories but that's it . . . and every time, you'd find it hard. She's just memories –

Zoya (*to* **Iqra**)   You were right.

Iqra   Zoya –

Zoya   How did I not see it?

Iqra   Nahi Zoya.

Zoya   Kya? –

Iqra   I'm leaving! –

Zoya   Kahaan? Where are you going?

Iqra   Home –

Zoya   Home?

Iqra *nods.*

Zoya   When will you be back?

Iqra *shakes her head.* **Zoya** *is shocked to her core. A beat. This pierces* **Zoya***'s heart.*

Zoya   Kab?

Iqra   In a few weeks.

A beat.

Iqra   I got into this programme in Karachi. Scholarship be hai. It's a year, and you can extend . . .

Zoya   What about your degree? You're quitting before you graduate? After all that work?

Iqra   I should've left a long time ago.

Zoya   Why didn't you, then! Go! Chal'na. Fuck off.

Faiza   Zoya, calm down.

Iqra   It's okay.

Zoya   What about your job? –

Iqra   This will help me get to where I need to be / what we talked about.

Zoya (*sarcastic*)   Musharaf's Pakistan will take you? What will you do in his government?

Iqra   It won't happen straight away, that would be naïve. I need to build myself.

Zoya   And then you'll do what he did to him? Kya ta? A 'coup d'état'? –

Iqra   Zoya. there's no place for me here. They treat me like shit, talk down to me like . . . I don't know anything, like –

Zoya   You're me. They talk to you as if you were me? Anparh. Mujhe patha hai.

Iqra   Nahi, Zoya. I didn't mean that. I can't stay here anymore.

Zoya   Why are you letting them scare you away. (*To* **Faiza**.) Tell her it gets better, go on, tell her!

Faiza   I don't think I can –

Zoya   There's more to look forward to, worth staying for, a whole new millennium, the 2000s, tell her.

Iqra   Zoya, I'm not scared . . . I'm exhausted.

A beat. **Iqra** *approaches* **Zoya**, *but* **Zoya** *recoils from her, pushing her away.* **Iqra**.

Knocks into the stock. Something drops.

Iqra   Zoya?

Zoya *picks it up. It could be the snow globe. She takes Woolies in. Over the course of this, she doesn't acknowledge the others –*

Zoya   I don't get it . . .

Iqra   Kya?

Zoya   People . . . *love* this place –

Iqra   They do –

Zoya   I thought they did –

Iqra   Of course they do –

Faiza   They always will!

Zoya   We've given so much to it, scrubbing floors, cleaning shelves, carrying stock – blood, sweat, tears . . . all for nothing, it'll go . . .

Iqra   Nahi, not for nothing, Zoya. You made it special for every single person who walked through that door.

Zoya   What does it matter now?

Iqra   And for me . . . you made it special for me. Zoya?

Zoya?

A beat. **Iqra** *tries to get closer to* **Zoya**, *but* **Zoya** *walks away from her.*

Iqra   Speak to me, na, Zoya?

Why won't you talk to me?

Iqra *tries to seek* **Zoya**'s *attention, but* **Zoya** *evades her, ignores her. For* **Faiza**, *it's all too familiar.*

Faiza   Give her time –

Iqra   Zoya? This isn't you.

Faiza   But it is. This is what she becomes.

Iqra *takes this in.* **Zoya** *stops still. She can hear water dripping. She sees a massive puddle, her dupatta floating on top of it. The snow woman has melted. She lifts it. Water drips from it. The* *leitmotif of Pardesi Pardesi appears, until it gets louder and louder. The moment distorts. She sings lyrics from the song.*

Zoya *abruptly faints.* **Faiza** *catches her in her arms – a trust hug that becomes a motherly embrace. The space gradually evolves into* **Faiza**'s *snow globe once more.*

Faiza   Mum? . . . It's okay. I've got you. You're okay.

Faiza *calmly positions* **Zoya** *on her back, her arms around her.*

Faiza *(touching her forehead)*   You're stone cold.

Faiza *kneels next to her and raises both her legs for a few moments.* **Zoya** *slowly regains consciousness.*

Faiza   I'm raising your legs, so they are above heart level. This will help you breathe – breathe, you'll be fine. You fainted. Your blood pressure dropped. Relax, you're fine.

Faiza *gradually lowers her legs, and crawls next to her, and helps her sit up –*

Faiza   How are you feeling? Are you feeling a little better?

Zoya *nods.* **Faiza** *passes her water.* **Zoya** *sips it.* **Faiza** *strokes her hair, wipes the sweat off her forehead.*

Faiza   Will you ever speak to me again? I wish I could just hear your voice again.

Zoya *takes* **Faiza** *in – something deeply softens in her. A beat.* **Zoya** *allows herself to be comforted.*

Faiza   You keep saying goodbye to the people you love. first them, your family, then her, Iqra . . . now, me.

Zoya *looks up to* **Faiza**. *What does this mean?*

Faiza   I'm not leaving you okay.

Faiza *holds the snow globe in her hand. It glows. Darkness surrounds them all, except the globe, which begins to glow against her face. Rather than snow, we see beams of colours rising upwards, the inverse of snow. She watches it in awe.*

Seven

(29ᵗʰ Dec) **Zoya** *and* **Iqra** *are working in Woolworths for what feels like the final time.* **Zoya** *eats some pick n mix.*

Iqra   Come with me.

A beat. **Zoya** *doesn't respond. She eats another sweet.*

Iqra   Whenever you can.

It doesn't need to be right now–

Zoya   Do you remember last Christmas that box of Quality Street, all the good ones had gone. Just the orange and strawberry creams were left, but buried deep beneath it, I see one blue one, my favourite, coconut wala, as I open it up there's lots of tiny wrappers inside –

Zoya *eats another.* **Iqra** *takes it out of her hand.*

Iqra   Stop that, Zoya –

Zoya   Kya? –

Iqra   This isn't you. (**Zoya** *takes this in.*)

What is it you said: 'we take responsibility for each other', look how low it is.

Zoya   It's what happens when you keep taking sweets, without paying, without refilling –

Iqra   I always make sure it's refilled –

Zoya   You can stop pretending you care about this place –

Iqra   I do care.

A beat.

Zoya   If she never said anything, would you ever tell me?

Iqra   Zoya? –

Zoya   Were you going to leave . . . without saying goodbye?

Iqra   The thought of seeing you hurt –

Zoya   My hurt would still be there whether you saw it or not, Iqra. You choose not to see it.

Iqra   I'm seeing it now, aren't I? You're seeing mine.

Zoya   I don't like this.

Iqra   Kya?

Zoya   The words coming out my mouth.

A beat.

Tumne sahee kaha ta.

This isn't me.

A beat. **Zoya** *tries to recompose herself.*

Iqra   This is what it was all for – you working here – so you could go back. Let's go back together.

Zoya   Did you not hear her?

Iqra   Mujhe patha hai.

Zoya   I stay. You go –

Iqra   It doesn't need to be that way. Why are you tormenting yourself like this –

Zoya   I belong here.

Iqra   None of us belong here, Zoya. Not even her. Why can't you see that?

Zoya   What happens to Jamal? I can't leave him –

Iqra   He can come too.

Zoya   His family is here, our family –

Iqra   They're not *your* family –

Zoya   Not yet –

Iqra   Your family is there, you miss them–

Zoya   What can Pakistan give us? How can it help us? (*Laughs.*)

Iqra   Kyu has-rahey-ho?

Zoya   When did you become so . . . naïve, Iqra?

Iqra   It's your home.

Zoya   Your privileges blind you. I can't just go back whenever I feel like it.

Iqra   Mein tumhay jaantee hoon –

Zoya   / Achaa?

Iqra   Like the veins in my palm –

Zoya   Allah has written my life. It stays here.

Iqra   Is that what you want?

Zoya   It will be, in time – Allah knows best.

Iqra   But right now . . . what does your heart say?

A beat. **Zoya** *turns to* **Faiza***, who appears, as in that first scene in the Woolies Christmas party –*

Zoya   Look at her.

Iqra   Kya?

A beat.

Zoya   She's perfect.

How can I ruin that? Her?

Iqra   You won't!

Zoya   Don't pretend you know my future.

Iqra   Why are you putting her life in front of your own?

Zoya   She's my life too, she's . . . my daughter –

Iqra   Because she saved your life?

Zoya Nahi, she doesn't need to do anything. My life is destined to be her mother, and yours is to go to Pakistan. Now we accept that as Allah's will.

Iqra Why are you being so . . . passive? This isn't you –

Zoya I married someone I barely knew, moved to a whole new country.

Iqra That's not passivity, Zoya – that's courage, faith, bravery.

Zoya And this isn't? I give her a good life, Iqra. I do something *right* with her. I'm not walking away from that.

Iqra Do you?

Zoya Kya matlab?

Iqra Is she happy? Really?

A beat. They stare at her.

Iqra Or does the denial in your heart – keeping yourself away from what you want, your pind, family – create a knot so hard it makes you . . . Resentful? Bitter? That you hurt the people you're meant to love.

Zoya I won't hurt her, ever.

Iqra I believe that –

Zoya Why would you say that? I'm not going to turn into her. I'll be a good mother–

Iqra Not an ounce of me doubts it –

Zoya I'll become a better one . . . now that I accept it with sukoon, sabr.

Iqra Are you ready, Zoya?

Zoya Is there anything in life we're ready for?

A beat.

Zoya   We change to the things Allah gives us, the blessings He gives us, we grow through them.

Iqra   It doesn't need to be this way – you can raise her in Pakistan, it takes a village, we know that – who will be your village here?

Zoya   Not you, we know that –

Iqra   Zoya.

Zoya   And it's okay, Iqra. Every path takes you to a new place . . . to beautiful things you couldn't dream of. I am excited for you. Why can't you be for me?

Iqra   I don't want to leave you here.

Zoya   I know –

Iqra   I'll miss you –

Zoya   You have better things ahead of you now.

Iqra   Nahi –

Zoya   You do, you will leave a mark, what did I say?

Iqra   The way you left a mark mere dil mein?

Zoya   Stop that –

Iqra   Kya? –

Zoya   When did you become so soft?

Iqra   I've spent too much time with you.

Zoya   A politician needs to be hard. Strong. Tough. You can't be soft Iqra.

Iqra   What will happen to you?

Zoya   I'll stay here.

Iqra   You can't stay *here*.

Zoya   When the time comes, I'll find somewhere else, you don't need to worry.

Iqra   I always will. This can't be the end Zoya.

Zoya   It doesn't need to be.

Iqra   I'll come back. I'll bring you here. I promise. We'll see Pakistan together – Gilgit, Karachi, Lahore, sub kuch – we'll make a new list –

Zoya *takes out the list from her purse, and the sad realisation that none of that will come to be hits her.* **Iqra** *glances at it.*

Iqra   And these last few days. Before I leave –

Zoya   It's not enough time –

Iqra   We can still make them special, make every moment count, theek hai?

Zoya   Theek hai. (*nods*) I'll try to savour all of this like those toffees we like . . .

But I don't think I can, not properly –

Iqra   Kyu?

Zoya   Knowing this will end.

Iqra   Zoya, look!

Iqra *points to* **Faiza**, *as one or two droplet of snow begin to fall. The pair step out into the cold, joining her. The three of them watch the snow fall from the sky. They touch it as it melts on their fingers.*

Eight

It's New Year's Eve. They're outside in their coats.

Faiza   You need to celebrate it, every year, promise me –

Zoya   Every Pakistani here was 'born' that day.

Faiza   And so were you –

Zoya   That's not true, we'll never know the real day.

Faiza   It doesn't take away from the day belonging to you –

Iqra We will celebrate your birthday zaroor – the moment midnight strikes, we will make it the best birthday you've ever had.

Faiza Promise me you will!

Zoya Achaa teek hai . . . why won't you celebrate it with me? where will you go?

Iqra She'll disappear, bilkul Cinderalla ki tarah – at midnight the spell will be broken.

Faiza I wish it was like that –

Zoya Already? you're leaving? (**Faiza** *nods.*)

Iqra Don't worry, she'll be back here, in nine months, popping out of you –

Zoya Bus kar yaar –

Faiza Why would you put it like that –

Iqra Kya? Isn't it true?

Zoya I can't get my head around it.

Faiza You'll be fine . . . just be yourself!

Zoya You make it sound so simple. I wish you could stay, tell me what to do.

Iqra How would that work –

Faiza I'm not leaving you – just this part of you.

Zoya To go back to the worse part of me –

Faiza No –

Iqra Not anymore –

Zoya How do I stop myself turning into her? . . .

Faiza Who?

Zoya The person you go back to –

Faiza   There's nothing wrong with her. I miss her . . . so much. I can't wait to see her again.

Zoya   Kyu?

Faiza   So I can show her I know how to love again . . . all the things you taught me here, what was in her all along –

Zoya   Nahi, you had that in you anyway / Faiza, what did I teach you?

Faiza   Because of you.

. . . What it means to be happy . . . to feel joy in your heart . . . Zoya.

Zoya   Hahn. Kya?

Faiza   Before I go, I need you to know that every time we go, we're not trying to hurt you, or punish you. But I know now how it feels like an act of leaving – like an act of betrayal . . . to someone who decided to stay, but we're not leaving you . . . not how your family left.

Zoya   I left them, Faiza –

Faiza   That's how it looked but that's not how it felt, is it? Not really –

Zoya   Why are you saying all this?

Faiza   We love you, and care about you more than anything in this world . . . but I don't think anything we do will ever repay what you've done for us, and even though we'll try, we'll fall short again and again . . . cos how can you give back to someone who left their country, their family for you? . . . To give you life?

A beat. **Zoya** *is touched.*

Zoya   Faiza. I want you to go.

Faiza   What?

Zoya   Go to Alaska, paint those dreamy skies.

Faiza   I can't, I'm not leaving you anymore.

Zoya   No you are, I want you to, okay, you listen to me. You live your life. Follow your dreams, every single one of them.

Faiza   Mum –

Zoya   Promise me, you will, Faiza.

Faiza *nods.*

Zoya (*turns to* **Iqra**)   And you –

Iqra   I'm not leaving you, Zoya.

Zoya   Stop lying to me. And yourself!

Iqra   Not here. (*Touches her heart.*) You'll always be here. I have something for you.

Iqra *passes* **Zoya** *bright pink tulips.*

Zoya   Pink tulips.

Iqra   Hanji.

A beat. **Zoya** *smells them. She lets* **Faiza** *smell them too –*

Faiza   They're gorgeous.

Zoya   Yeh kyu? Am I dying?

Iqra   Tauba karru.

Faiza   No one is dying, you'll be okay, you both will –

Iqra   How do you know? You don't know where I am, I could've been assassinated –

Zoya   Achaaa? you think that much of yourself.

Iqra   Chupp'nee.

Faiza   We'll find you, together (*turns to* **Zoya**), the moment I get back I'll put the hob on and make us a big pot of chai, and then we'll talk like we've not talked in months . . . and then I promise you, we'll go Pakistan and we'll find her.

Iqra   That's if we haven't beaten you to it. We made intentions. We made a list.

A beat. **Zoya** *looks up at* **Iqra** *– this is the end, and it sinks in for her.*

Zoya (*to* **Iqra**)   Tussi jaa rahe ho?

Tussi na jao.

Iqra *laughs behind tears.*

Iqra   Tum yaad rakhna kahin bhool na jaana.

Zoya   How could I forget you, Iqra Razwan? Even if we never find each other –

Iqra   Don't say that –

Zoya   I want you to be happy, okay? –

We can hear the distant ring of bells.

Faiza   It's time –

Zoya   Already? I haven't said everything that I needed to say –

Faiza   It's okay, we have so much time–

Zoya   It's come too soon. If for some reason she never says it . . . if you never hear me say it, Faiza, thank you –

Faiza   What for? –

Zoya   For giving me life.

Faiza's *heart swells, she reaches for her mother's hand.* **Zoya** *clasps it, then kisses it.*

Then **Zoya** *reaches for* **Iqra**'s *hand. The three hold each other's hands, as the bell continues its last few dings, and they watch the fireworks – bright flares of light shoot, blinding them and us, and as darkness returns, 'Auld Lang Syne' plays, and* **Faiza** *is no longer there.*

Zoya *and* **Iqra** *are in the new millennium. They glance at one another, as it continues playing.*

Zoya   Happy New Year!

Iqra   Happy Birthday, meri jaan.

Iqra *leans her head against* **Zoya***'s and wraps her arms around her. Darkness.*

.